The Book of the Rose

The Book of the Rose

DAVID SQUIRE WITH JANE NEWDICK

CRESCENT BOOKS
New York

A SALAMANDER BOOK

This 1991 edition first published by Crescent Books,
distributed by Outlet Book Company, Inc., A Random House Company,
225 Park Avenue South, New York, New York 10003.

© Salamander Books 1991

ISBN: 0-517-05913-4

8   7   6   5   4   3   2   1

CREDITS

Editor: Lisa Dyer
Designer: Bridgewater Design Ltd.
Photographer: Di Lewis
Illustrator: Vana Haggerty
Color Reproduction: Scantrans, Pte Ltd., Singapore

Printed in Hong Kong

Contents

Introduction

The rose reigns supreme over all the other flowers in the plant kingdom. It has always held an important place in literature and legend, romance and everyday life, art and fashion. From Roman times when baskets of rose petals were strewn ankle deep for the delight of emperors and their guests, to the rose as the humble ingredient of scented recipes and sumptuous perfumes, this special flower has twined and blossomed its way through history like no other.

Whether it is the small delicate single flowers of the wild Dog Rose or the rich and densely petalled heads of a Bourbon or Centifolia, the rose always thrills and delights us with its unsurpassed combination of scent, colour and perfect form.
For all its delicacy of flower, the rose is a hardy and long-lived plant. Able to withstand quite rugged and difficult conditions it still manages to regularly produce a cornucopia of blooms, from what appears to be an unpromising and often wickedly thorny stem. Tumbling masses of flowers bloom for a week or two in midsummer, or, in some cases, for many fruitful months.

In The Romance of the Rose, you will discover both the history and mystique which surround the rose. Long a symbol of beauty and love, the rose has inspired centuries of painters, writers and poets who have immortalized this beloved flower. The rose has been cherished and carefully cultivated throughout time, not only for its value as a garden plant but also for its uses in medicines, perfumes, foods and as a motif on fabrics and china.

The many different decorative and useful aspects of the rose are explored in A Bouquet of Roses. There are ideas for exquisite but simple flower arrangements as well as ways to prolong the beauty of summer roses long into the winter by making pot-pourris, scented sachets, garlands and both sweet and savoury foods. The rose has been highly valued for its long lasting and sweet perfume and this chapter offers both new and traditional ideas to exploit this aspect of the rose.

The best source of roses is, of course, your own garden. Because plant breeders throughout the last few centuries have used their skills to combine different roses from all over the world, we now have a rich heritage of roses from which to choose. A Glossary of Roses is invaluable for identifying and choosing the types of rose that will suit you and your environment. There is also a special listing on rose scents and colours and there are helpful tips for caring for garden roses.

Painting of a flower seller by the artist George Lawrence Bulleid (1858–1933). This painting includes the rose as a romantic symbol.

The Romance of the Rose

The rose is the ultimate romantic image. At the mere mention of the word, thoughts often turn to a single beautiful red bloom, perhaps displayed exquisitely in an elegant silver vase. It is not surprising that we associate the rose with red, as the word 'rose' is derived through the Latin and Greek from a Celtic word meaning 'red'. But why should this garden shrub be so popular? And why are the many facets of this flower woven so finely into our heritage and lives?

Perhaps it is because the rose is a wonderful symbol for life and love. A rose with thorns displays the paradox of beauty and pain, of the birth of the bloom with the death inherent in the thorn. The rose has been used throughout the ages to symbolize youth, love, romance, sexuality, purity and perfect beauty. A true symbol of the human condition, it is no wonder the rose has played such an important part in human life.

The rose has long been a source of inspiration; poems and song lyrics extol its virtues, and artists depict its rich sensuality on canvas. It has been popularly used to woo women throughout time; in courtship, the giving of a bouquet of roses represents the giving of love. Even manufacturers and advertisers have recognized its sales potential. Its name has been used to describe architectural features, such as rose windows, as well as other plants which have attributes of the rose, such as rosewood. Medicines are made more palatable by its addition, coins are imprinted with its image, it is even a popular female Christian name. Almost everywhere we look, we can find evidence of the rose.

In this section, the many facets of this spectacular flower are paraded, revealing its influence upon our lives. The breadth and detailed nature of roses in human life is so vast that to encompass just a distillation of it in anything smaller than several sets of encyclopedias is impossible. Therefore, this first section is a pot-pourri of rose history, folklore, literature, lyrics and paintings.

This painting, Yellow and Pink Roses of Bengal, by Pierre-Joseph Redouté (1759–1840), is from Les Choix des Plus Belles Fleurs.

This still-life of roses, lilies and strawberries is by François Charette-Duval (1836–1878). Fruit, as well as butterflies and birds, were a typical feature of flower paintings of this period.

A History of the Rose

Ancient Days

Fossilized leaves found in North America, France, Germany, Japan and Czechoslovakia suggest that roses were in existence some four million years ago, preceding Man's presence by many years. During the early part of the 1900s, Sir Arthur John Evans was excavating on the site of the royal palace of Minos at Knossos, Crete, which is acclaimed as Europe's earliest civilization. The frescoes and broken pieces of pottery that he uncovered revealed that roses, together with irises, lilies and crocuses, were cultivated in about 1800BC. The rose depicted on these Minoan frescoes is the Damascene or Damask Rose (*Rosa damascena*), a hybrid of *Rosa gallica*, the French or Provins Rose, and *Rosa phoenicea*. This hybrid is said to have been taken to Abyssinia by early Christians and planted near their churches. Forms of the hybrid were taken back to western Europe, especially France, by returning Crusaders.

Ancient gardens in Persia abounded with roses that became so popular that the Persian word for 'rose' and 'flower' was the same, with the violet known as 'the prophet of the rose'. The Persians adored flowers and trees, and it is said that the western love of plants is derived from this Persian influence. Indeed, the word 'paradise' comes from the Persian word for park or garden. The rose was brought from Persia to Babylon, where it became a symbol of state power, joining the eagle and apple on the staff of office.

Growing roses became popular in China as early as 500BC. The Imperial Chinese library houses an extensive collection of books about the flower. Confucius especially mentions rose gardens in Peking.

Roses were also held in high esteem in Central Asia: the Hindu goddess Lakshmi – thought to be the most beautiful woman of India and renowned for good fortune, love and beauty – is said to have been born from a rose formed of 108 large and 1008 small rose petals.

The rose was honoured in ancient Greece and Rome with gardens in Cyrene and Rhodes devoted to it. Sappho, a Greek lyrical poet about 600BC and at the centre of a feminine literary coterie at Mytilene, called the rose the 'queen of flowers'.

In classical Greek mythology, the rose is well associated with Aphrodite, the Greek goddess of love, wedlock and fertility. According to legend, her priestesses were clothed in wreaths of white roses, and their paths scattered with roses.

In the Republic of Rome, wreaths were formed of roses, unlike the laurels of Greece. Military valour was acknowledged by roses and it was a great honour for the VIII Legion when permission was granted for a rose to be emblazoned on its shield in recognition of conquering Africa.

The Rose of Rhodes, on the reverse of this Greek didrahm, is evidence of the popularity of the rose in ancient times, circa 200BC.

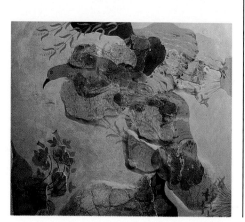

The Roses and Blue Birds frescoe, which was found by Sir Arthur John Evans at Knossos, Crete, is one of the earliest examples of roses, circa 1600–1800BC.

Roses played a ceremonial part in acknowledging military valour during the Roman Republic. In this painting by Sir Lawrence Alma-Tadema (1836–1912), Caracallia, a Roman emperor, fights his rival, his brother Geta.

Rose wreaths were formed of rose petals threaded in an overlapping pattern, creating a thick roll. The giving of rose wreaths for easy success or just for decoration was resisted. Indeed, a money-lender who wore a wreath-crown of roses was thrown in jail by order of the Senate. In the later days of the Republic, floral wreaths became more common and eventually there arose the custom of young men wearing wreaths of roses when attending councils, as well as when going into battle.

During the reign of Augustus and about the time of the birth of Jesus Christ, roses were widely used for house decoration, as well as on tombs. However, they were essentially flowers of love and festivals. Lovers exchanged rose wreaths and young and old alike wore crowns of roses, while dancing girls, musicians and cup-bearers were also bedecked. It was even customary while proposing a toast to a friend to pluck rose petals from a head wreath and to drop them in the wine.

Flowers were also eaten, and rose wine was taken with meals. Roman recipes dating from this period instruct on making main dishes and wine using roses. Indeed, there seems to have been no limit to the uses invented for the rose.

ROMAN DISH

Pound rose petals
in the mortar and sieve them;
add four calve's brains, pepper, salt,
eight eggs, a glass and a half of
good wine and a few spoonfuls of oil.
Bake in the oven in a mould greased with oil.

ROMAN ROSE WINE

Thread together rose petals from
which the white part has been removed
and steep them in wine for seven days.
Then take them out of the wine and in the
same way put in other fresh rose petals
threaded together, for another seven days.
Repeat a third time, then strain
the wine and add honey.

Roses increasingly became a sign of lavish living. Shiploads of roses were imported from Alexandria, on the North African coast, while in Rome greenhouses roofed in selenite (gypsum in the form of colourless clear crystals) and heated by hot-water pipes, ensured roses could be flowered in winter.

Petal-filled cushions were popular, as well as fine-meshed bags packed with petals and hung around the neck and nose. This rose luxury is said to have been given popularity by Cleopatra in Egypt, when she seduced Mark Antony. Rooms knee-deep in roses, mattresses and cushions packed with petals, and fountains filled with rose water were not uncommon.

The Roman poet, Horace, observed that the fertile fields of Italy were being turned into rose gardens; olive trees were being neglected in favour of roses and violets. At about the same time, Pliny, the Roman scholar, relates:

today the material for wreaths comes from India or from yet more distant countries. The most highly prized wreaths are made of Indian nard (which grows in the central Himalayas) or interwoven with fine silks and dripping with scented ointments. That's how extravagant our womenfolk have become!

The trend towards opulent living was damaging the Roman economy, encouraging the poet and writer Martial to observe:

Send us wheat, O Egyptians, we shall send you roses in return.

By the time Domitian was emperor in 81AD the smell of roses in Rome was said to be overpowering.

The Roses of Heliogabalus, also by Sir Lawrence Alma-Tadema, shows roses as a decadent element in the Roman emperor's festivities.

—— Medieval Times ——

By the Middle Ages, roses were in abundance in England. The exact introduction of roses into Britain is unknown. However, the Old Rose, *Rosa alba*, may have arrived in Britain via Roman traders. This particular rose became popular and was incorporated into the Great Seal of State by Edward I. The Damask Rose, from western Asia, is thought to have been introduced into Britain by traders or monks, but mainly by returning Crusaders.

Edward I, who died in 1307, had a great interest in plants. In 1275 his garden at the Tower of London was planted with several hundred roses as well as a multitude of vine stocks, cherry trees, willows, peonies, lilies and peach and quince trees. Records of the time indicate that many plants were being bought or exchanged. In 1255 Edward had married Queen Eleanor of Castile, herself a keen gardener, who employed two gardeners brought to Kings Langley in England from Aragon (once an independent kingdom in north-eastern Spain).

During this period, roses were cultivated for their supposed medicinal attributes as well as for their beauty. In 1306 the Damask

During the Middle Ages in Europe, roses were abundantly grown in gardens. This French manuscript illustration, circa 1465 and entitled Emilia in Her Garden, offers a view of the time period.

This woodcut, from an early edition of Gerard's The Herball, shows the Damask Rose in detail.

influential *The Herball, or generall historie of plantes* in 1597. This book featured the rose, along with many other plants, and offered practical botanical information as well as folklore.

Another medieval use for roses was in the making of mead, a traditional honey and water drink popular with the ancient Greeks and early Britons. It is still brewed in Great Britain today.

Empress Josephine and —— Malmaison ——

In the nineteenth century, roses were important features in the gardens of royalty and the upper classes.

Josephine, Empress of France from 1804 to 1809 and first wife of Napoleon Boneparte, made a large collection of wild and cultivated roses at her favourite château at Malmaison, Hauts-de-Seine, which Napoleon purchased and she acquired in 1798. The garden was very much in the English style, in part

Many artists captured the beauty of the rose on canvas in the nineteenth century. Henri Fantin-Latour (1836–1904) reveals the delicacy of the flower in his Pink and White Roses.

Rose was mentioned in Edward I's *Bill of Medicines*. Later, a syrup made from an infusion of its petals was thought to benefit the bowels. Rose and violet syrups were widely prescribed against many ailments, including fevers, but the central role of these elixirs was to make some of the more disagreeable medieval remedies more palatable!

Other roses with medicinal qualities were also grown, such as *Rosa rubiginosa*, the Sweet-briar or Eglantine. As a modern medicine it has little value, but in 1649 Nicholas Culpepper published *The Complete Herbal*, mentioning that the spongy apples found upon the Eglantine could be used to cure alopecia. Apparently, they were pounded to a paste and mixed with honey and wood ash before being applied to the scalp. The earlier herbalist, John Gerard, had published the

Although Josephine's Malmaison garden is long gone, the 'Souvenir de la Malmaison' remains as a nostalgic reminder of that most majestic garden.

formed of a series of flower beds. This stylized design was later to be called *gardenesque* rather than *picturesque*.

Violets played an important role in Napoleon's life, but Josephine's delight was roses. She engaged the creator of the rose garden at the Luxembourg Gardens, Paris, to collect all known kinds of roses, resulting in Malmaison becoming the most famous rose garden of its time.

An amusing anecdote about a French garden tells how the name of one rose kept changing, rivalling the Vicar of Bray who, in the sixteenth century, repeatedly changed religions according to the sovereign then reigning. During the so-called Hundred Days, between Napoleon's return from Elba and his exile to St Helena, a rose bred at St Cloud was called 'Rose de l'Empereur', but when Louis XVIII was enthroned it was renamed 'Rose du Roi'. Later it became 'Crimson Perpetual'.

Napoleon's armies were instructed to collect and send to Malmaison roses from wherever they were found. Even during hostilities, roses were given safe passage. The British Admiralty gave orders that if a ship carrying plants or seeds for Malmaison was seized, the botanical treasures should be sent immediately to Malmaison.

John Kennedy of the Vineyard Nursery at Hammersmith, near London, was sum-

moned by the Empress to advise on the planting of her garden. Subsequently, he frequently travelled between London and France, in spite of the Napoleonic Wars then in progress. He had a special botanical charge d'affaires pass that allowed him unchallenged passage in order to buy roses for Josephine. The Empress spent enormous sums of money on her garden and left debts, it is said, in excess of 2,500,000 francs.

Josephine engaged the services of many eminent botanists and gardeners, including Aimé Bonpland who supervised the gardens from 1806. She also engaged famous artists to depict Malmaison. The garden was immortalized by Pierre-Joseph Redouté, a Belgian artist working in France, in his 'Jardin de Malmaison'. Redouté's name is now forever remembered for his detailed paintings of French Old Roses, which have been reproduced many times and appear in a variety of forms, from fine art prints to calendars.

After Josephine's death in 1814, the gardens were neglected and, in 1828, eventually sold by auction, together with the palace. About 1896 Daniel Osiris bought the gardens, had them restored and in 1904 gave them to the French government.

The glory of Malmaison is remembered in the recurrent-flowering Climber 'Souvenir de la Malmaison', with delicately scented, blush-coloured blooms up to 13cm (5in) across. Several stories exist about its origination, including that it was grown by Beluze who mysteriously sent it, unnamed, to Malmaison in 1843, after Josephine's death and when the gardens were neglected. It was admired by a visiting Russian Grand Duke who returned with it as a souvenir to the Imperial Gardens at St Petersburg.

The gardens at one time covered 1726 hectares (1793 acres) but are now very much reduced in size. However, a section is set aside for the cultivation of roses, for which it was famed.

Contemporary Rose Gardens

Although the beauty of the original Malmaison garden has been lost (except in art), there are many modern gardens which capture the majesty of roses in bloom. Rose gardens have been developed in many parts of the world, and especially in Europe, Great Britain and North America. They offer a wide range of types and varieties. Rose nurseries, worldwide, also offer the opportunity to see both established and new varieties.

In the United States, a public rose garden has been established since 1904 at Elizabeth Park, Connecticut, while in Portland, Oregon, there is the International Rose Test Garden which presents many new roses. The Hershey Rose Garden in Pennsylvania offers a wide range of roses, from those in beds to Ramblers and Climbers.

In Ontario, Canada, the Centennial Rose Gardens in Burlingham offer trials of hardiness, as well as more than 450 old and established varieties and about 3000 newer ones.

The Queen Mary Rose Garden at Regents Park in London exhibits a fine collection of Old Roses. Here, the pink roses are displayed on a grandiose scale.

The British Isles are rich in rose collections, including the Royal National Rose Society's gardens at St Albans, Hertfordshire. This society, initially the National Rose Society, was founded in 1876 and has markedly benefited roses. Interestingly, the society's gardens are arranged in the same *gardenesque* style as the one made famous by Empress Josephine at Malmaison. They contain examples of all types of roses, both old types and new hybrids.

In London, the Queen Mary Rose Garden in Regent's Park is worth visiting, as is Mottisfont Abbey, near Romsey, Hampshire, where the National Trust has a superb collection of Old Roses.

In France, Paris houses several superb rose gardens, including Bagatelle, in the Bois de Boulogne, and La Roseraie de l'Hay les Roses which is rich in Climbers.

Germany has the Sangerhausen Rosarium, near Leipzig, opened just after the turn of the century and now accommodating some 6500 species and varieties.

Pictured here is the Temple de L'Amour, decorated with climbing roses, in the Roseraie de l'Hay les Roses in Paris.

Wars and Roses

Roses have been associated with wars, both secular and religious. In the Crusades, the rose featured as a sacred Muslim symbol. In the Wars of the Roses, perhaps the best-known wars associated with roses, the roses were emblems of two opposing families vying for the English throne.

—— Religious Crusades ——

During the eleventh, twelfth and thirteenth centuries, military expeditions were undertaken by many European Christians to recover the Holy Land from the Muslims.

A portrait of the Sultan Mohammed II, from fifteenth century Byzantine, pictures him with a red rose, a sacred symbol to Muslims during the Crusades.

In 1187, when Saladin, the Sultan of Egypt, conquered Jerusalem, he sent 500 camels laden with rose water for cleaning the Omar mosque, named after Omar, an Arabian Caliph who was one of Mohammed's ablest advisers. Saladin had been engaged by the Atabeg of Mosul to recover Jerusalem from the Christians. This precipitated the Third Crusade led by Richard I, the Lionheart, of England. It failed, and in 1192 Saladin and Richard made peace.

The rose was sacred to all Muslims, and by washing the mosque in rose water they cleansed it of Christian beliefs. It was so prized that newborn babies of the seraglio, a sultan's women's palace, were wrapped in rose petals, later in rose-coloured gauze. Indeed, as late as 1750, Turkey and Egypt were importing hundreds of bales of this material.

In 1453, the Turkish sultan Mohammed II captured Christian Constantinople (once Byzantium, capital of the Byzantine Empire, and now Istanbul). The magnificent church of St Sophia had been founded by Justinian the Great in 532AD and dedicated on Christmas Day 538AD. When Mohammed II arrived it was changed to a mosque, and he had it purified with rose water, just as Saladin had cleansed the Omar mosque some three hundred years earlier.

Before Mohammed II's arrival, Constantinople had a strong Greek influence and the wearing of white roses in wreaths was common and according to ancient custom. To the Turks, however, the white rose had its origin in Mohammed's drops of perspiration during his ascension. For white roses to be worn by non-believers, and with the chance of white petals falling to the ground, was taken to be an insult. One procession of rose-wreathed inhabitants was even massacred for the offence.

—— The Wars of the Roses ——

The Wars of the Roses, for possession of the English throne, were between the supporters of the House of York and the House of Lan-

This etching depicts the legendary start of the Wars of the Roses. Here, the Dukes of York and Lancaster meet near roses in the Temple Gardens.

caster. The Yorkists had a white rose as their emblem, probably *Rosa alba semi-plena*, while the Lancastrians had the old red Damask Rose, *Rosa gallica* 'Officinalis', also known as the Apothecary's Rose and the Red Rose of Lancaster.

These roses were emblems of the two families long before the Wars of the Roses. A white rose was the emblem of Eleanor of Provence who, in 1235, married Henry III. Her emblem subsequently descended to her son, Edward I. The Red Rose of Lancaster was acquired by Edmund, the second son of Henry III, through his marriage in 1275 to Blanche, widow of Henry I of France (known as Henry the Fat).

The Wars are said to have been sparked off by a quarrel in the Temple Gardens – an area in London between Fleet Street and the River Thames – in 1455. In *Henry VI: Part I, Act II, Sc. iv*, written about one and a half centuries later, William Shakespeare sets a scene, concerning the quarrel, between Richard Plantagenet and Somerset.

PLANTAGENET Let him that is a true-born gentleman,
And stands upon the honour of his birth,
If he suppose that I have pleaded truth,
From off this brier pluck a white rose with me.

SOMERSET Let him that is no coward nor no flatterer,
But dare maintain the part of the truth,
Pluck a red rose from off this thorn with me.

[Various supporters then choose their roses too]

PLANTAGENET Now, Somerset, where is your argument?

SOMERSET Here, in my scabbard; meditating that
Shall dye your white rose in a bloody red.

PLANTAGENET Meantime, your cheeks do counterfeit our roses;
For pale they look with fear, as witnessing
The truth on our side.

SOMERSET No, Plantagenet,
'Tis not for fear but anger that thy cheeks
Blush for pure shame to counterfeit our roses,
And yet thy tongue will not confess thy error.

The start of the Wars of the Roses can be traced back many years before the onset of the fighting. Richard II, who followed his grandfather Edward III as king in 1377, was deposed and succeeded in 1399 by his Lancastrian cousin, Henry IV, another grandson of Edward III. For four generations the factions of the royal family and their attendant nobles plotted, argued and fought for supremacy, with many changing sides more than once – notoriously Warwick, the Kingmaker. By the middle of the fifteenth century all attempts at compromise had failed and in 1455 the Wars began.

The ensuing battles – including St Albans, Towton, Hexham and Tewkesbury – were fierce and bloody. It is said that in the course of the Wars there perished twelve princes of the blood, two hundred nobles and 100,000 gentry and common people.

With the ascension of Edward IV to the throne in 1460 it seemed for a while that the Yorkists had gained the final victory, but ten years later his position was threatened once more and Lancaster's Henry VI returned briefly to the throne before being beaten again by Edward IV at Barnet, just north of London.

Edward IV was succeeded by his brother, Richard III, and the long struggle ended on 22nd August 1485, with the defeat and death of Richard III on Bosworth Field. The battle's victor, Henry Tudor, obscurely related to both factions but with a tenuous claim to the throne, imposed a peace which was sealed by his political marriage the following year to Elizabeth of York, daughter of Edward IV. The Tudor rose, adopted by Henry's son, Henry VIII, symbolized this union of the two houses by combining the petals of the Red Rose of Lancaster and the White Rose of York. Henry VIII had this red and white rose incorporated into his coat of arms.

A red and white rose, *Rosa damascena* 'Versicolor', is thought to have been discovered in a monastery in Wiltshire in the fifteenth century, and in 1551 is said to have taken the name York and Lancaster Rose. Many historical accounts of the beginning of the Wars say that the quarrel took place around a bush of this rose. It is a beautiful shrub, with somewhat untidy, fragrant, semi-double flowers during June and July.

Confusion has existed between *Rosa damascena* 'Versicolor' and another red and white rose, 'Rosa Mundi' (*Rosa gallica* 'Versicolor'). The distinction is clear, in that 'Rosa Mundi' forms a smaller shrub, and reveals bright, showy flowers, crimson striped or splashed with blush-white. It has also erroneously gained the name York and Lancaster Rose from its apparent combination of the individual colours of the two rose emblems.

Henry VIII's shield of arms, from a sixteenth-century stained glass window, shows the red and white roses which were combined in the coat of arms after the Wars.

One of the many bloody wars in the Wars of the Roses was at Barnet, here depicted on a manuscript dating from 1470.

Folklore, Legend and Everyday Sayings

—— An Origin of the Rose ——

Sir John Mandeville (also known as Maundeville) lived during the fourteenth century and was well known for his travel books. Unfortunately, his reputation for truth became tainted, as he was later known for his highly inventive lies.

In one legend, he colourfully reveals that the first roses appeared miraculously at Bethlehem. He tells that a Jewish maid of Bethlehem (said by Robert Southey in the nineteenth century to be called Zillah) was beloved by Hamuel, a brutish sot. Hamuel's love was rejected and he vowed vengeance, saying that Zillah was demonic. She was condemned to be burnt at the stake but as a result of prayers God averted the flames and the stake budded into a rose tree. The young maid stood unharmed under a canopy of white and red roses, reputed to be the first seen on earth since Paradise was lost.

—— Aphrodite and Adonis ——

In classical mythology and fine art paintings, the rose is often associated with Aphrodite, the Greek goddess of love (the Romans called the goddess Venus).

In one myth, Adonis, a beautiful youth beloved by Aphrodite for his striking looks, lay mortally wounded by a wild boar. Aphrodite hurried to his side, rushing through a thorny hedge, the white roses being tinged red by her blood, while Adonis himself was transformed into an anemone.

Botticelli's famous Birth of Venus depicts the goddess of love (also called Aphrodite by the Greeks) surrounded by pink roses.

St Valentine's Day was named for St Valentine, here painted on glass. However, this celebration also owes its tradition to the Roman festival of Lupercalia.

customary for just the man to give cards and presents, but now both sexes offer their sweethearts cards and presents. Why these should be given anonymously is unknown, but perhaps recalls the excitement of the love urn in Roman times, when there was an uncertainty of the maiden selected.

Rather unromantically, it is also thought that 'Valentine' may be a corruption of *galantin* (the French word for a lover or dangler), and that St Valentine was chosen solely because of his name.

Rhymes recording the festival of St Valentine are many, and several include references to roses.

—— St Valentine's Day ——
The rose features in many rhymes associated with St Valentine's Day, a celebration which came about when a popular pagan custom merged with Christianity. Valentine's Day is now well known as a day when lovers declare themselves, usually anonymously.

The pre-Christian Roman festival of Lupercalia, celebrated on February 15th, involved the sacrifice of dogs and goats, with priests wandering around carrying goatskin thongs, a blow from which was believed to cure the barrenness of women. It is also reported to have been a mating ritual: names or tokens of young, marriageable girls were put into a love urn, local boys taking a name and pairing with the named maiden.

St Valentine was a Christian priest in Roman times, martyred under Claudius II for his faith on February 14th, about 271AD. St Julius I, then bishop of Rome, canonized him in about 337AD, built a church in his memory and nominated February 14th St Valentine's Day.

When Christianity arrived in Britain, the mating festival was moved to the 14th, merging the two festivals. At one time it was

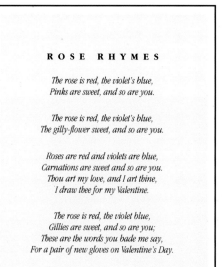

ROSE RHYMES

The rose is red, the violet's blue,
Pinks are sweet, and so are you.

The rose is red, the violet's blue,
The gilly-flower sweet, and so are you.

Roses are red and violets are blue,
Carnations are sweet and so are you.
Thou art my love, and I art thine,
I draw thee for my Valentine.

The rose is red, the violet blue,
Gillies are sweet, and so are you;
These are the words you bade me say,
For a pair of new gloves on Valentine's Day.

—— Charlemagne's Rose Tree ——
One legend tells that over a thousand years ago Charlemagne, also known as Charles the Great, planted a rose tree in the cloisters of Hildesheim Cathedral, a town in Lower Saxony (Germany) and at the foot of the Harz Mountains.

Evidence of this particular rose tree was recorded more than 500 years ago. Then, in 1884, the tree's growth diminished and on investigation it was found that the roots were covered with debris. This was removed and

century, Queen Eleanor of Aquitaine, who was Henry II's wife, murdered Rosamund with a poison, while visiting her on the pretense of offering silken thread.

—— St Elizabeth of Hungary ——

St Elizabeth was born in the beginning of the thirteenth century. She was known for her generosity towards the poor and sick, and founded several hospices. In legend, she is on an errand for the poor when she meets her husband. The loaves of bread she is carrying are transformed into roses, convincing her husband of the worthiness of her charitable endeavours.

—— Fairy Tales ——

Many traditional fairy tales include stories of the rose. Among the most famous is Beauty and the Beast. In this story, a father

Evelyn De Morgan (1855–1918), in his painting Queen Eleanor and Fair Rosamund, depicts the legendary murder of Rosamund.

replaced by fresh soil, and drains were installed to ensure a regular supply of rainwater to the roots.

During the Second World War, in the spring of 1945, the historic part of the city, including the cathedral, was devastated. It is said that, although much of the growth was damaged, the roots of this same rose tree were safe and that within six months fresh growth had attained a height of 3.5 m (12 ft).

Rosamund and Queen
—— Eleanor ——

In the middle of the twelfth century, Rosamund was the mistress of Henry II, and was a very fair and lovely lady. Many early legends about her exist, and some story-tellers play on her name, using the connection to roses. In medieval tales dating from the fourteenth

This stained glass window from the Church of St Mary in Sturminster Newton, Durham, and by Harry Clarke of Dublin, shows St Elizabeth of Hungary with her arms full of roses.

The Sleeping Princess, by Sir Edward Burne-Jones, shows briar roses growing over the princess as she lies spellbound.

asks his three daughters what gift they would like best. His youngest answers that she would like a simple gift, a red rose.

After searching the world over he finds himself in a castle with exquisite gardens, among which is the most beautiful red rose he has ever seen. He steals the rose, but is met by a Beast who demands his life for the theft. Eventually the Beast falls in love with the youngest daughter and is transformed into a prince.

Sleeping Beauty is another well-known fairy tale. A princess is spellbound to sleep until a prince awakens her with a kiss. During the hundred years of her sleep, roses and thorns grow up around the castle, hiding it from view.

—— Rosaries ——

The naming and derivation of rosaries, used by Roman Catholics to keep count of their repetitions of certain prayers, are many: from the chaplet of beads perfumed by roses and given by the Virgin Mary to St Dominic; from

The rosary was probably named after the monastic gardens in the Middle Ages which were called rosaries. Pictured here is a seventeenth century Italian rosary made of carved boxwood beads.

24

St Rosalie's name; and from original rose-wood beads.

However, it is clear that the oldest meaning of rosary is that of a rose garden; an enclosed rosary being the perfect place for devotions to the Virgin Mary. The connection between the rose garden and Christian rosary beads was thought to have been made in Europe during the twelfth century.

Much earlier, Irish monks had given psalter singing an important place in devotions by separating psalms into three sets of fifty. By 1050 they were making strings of beads, sometimes in circles, to aid counting. It was not until the thirteenth century that these beads were first called a rosary, by Thomas of Cantipre (or Cantimpre).

—— Rosy Misconceptions ——

Many plants have 'rose' as part of their name, but, in fact, bear little or no resemblance to garden roses. Rosewood does not belong to any *Rosa* species, but belongs to a group of tropical and sub-tropical trees with hard, reddish or dark wood with strongly marked grain. It is so named because, when cut, the wood has the fragrance of roses.

—— Ring-a-Ring o' Roses ——

This is a popular chant with children, but it is said to have originated at the time of the Great Plague, prevalent in London about 1664. The ring of roses is the rosy mark on the skin, indicating a victim of the plague. The full jingle is:

> *Ring-a-ring o' roses*
> *A pocket full of posies;*
> *Atishoo, atishoo, we all fall down.*

The 'pocket full of posies' referred to a mixture of herbs carried by people to ward off the plague, while 'Atishoo, atishoo' referred to one of the symptoms. 'We all fall down', of course, meant that the victim had

collapsed, with the sad prospect of death, which often came quickly. The disease was rapidly spread by the fleas of rats; unfortunately, dogs and cats were thought to spread the plague and were killed, so removing the main chance of destroying rats.

—— A Bed of Roses ——

This is a well-known saying from Christopher Marlowe, a contemporary of William Shakespeare, who in 'The Passionate Shepherd to his Love' wrote:

> *And I will make thee beds of roses,*
> *And a thousand fragrant posies.*

This implies that anyone 'on a bed of roses' is having a happy and comfortable time. An earlier reference to a bed of roses is said to apply to the people of Sybaris, (an ancient Greek city in southern Italy that was destroyed in 510BC) who slept in luxury on mattresses filled with rose petals.

The enactment of the rhyme 'Ring-a-ring 'o roses' has here been charmingly captured by the nineteenth-century artist Harriet M. Bennet.

—— Sub Rosa ——

Sub rosa, or 'under the rose', means in strict confidence. It is said that Cupid gave Harpocrates (the god of silence) a rose to bribe him not to betray the amours of Venus. Indeed, an anonymous Latin poet wrote:

The rose is the flower of Venus: in order that her sweet thefts might be concealed, Love dedicated to Harpocrates, the God of Silence, this gift of his mother. Hence the host hangs over his friendly table a rose, that the guests underneath it may know how to keep silence as to what is said.

The custom spread to England and was widely used during the days of chivalry. Indeed, the practice of placing rose emblems over confessionals in Roman Catholic churches began in 1523, during the office of Pope Adrian VI.

Rose motifs are also widely used in church architecture, and many cathedrals, such as York and Exeter in England, have beautifully wrought examples. Masonic lodges of the Middle Ages also used the rose as a symbol of secrecy because, it is said, the outer parts

Ernest Ludolf Meyer painted these briars of wild pink roses during the late nineteenth century.

of a rose in bud display the pentagram or Druid's foot, a secret countersign of Pythagoreans. It was also a sacred symbol for the Celts and frequently used on Gallic coins. Additionally, the five-sided symbol had importance for the Turks, who believed that the rose held the five secrets of Allah.

In Victorian times the rose was widely used to convey amorous messages, here again the suggestion being that it was in secret. In many Victorian dining rooms the decorative plaster motif in the ceiling above the table was called a rose, implying that anything said at the table was in confidence and should not be repeated.

Although the symbolic purpose of the rose may no longer be heeded, these ceiling decorations are still referred to as roses, even when reduced to a plastic ring around a light wire.

The Grant Rose and other American —— Legends ——

America also abounds with rose legends, including the scented Grant Rose which is said to have arisen from the blood of Mrs Grant, an early settler, killed by the Seminole Indians of Florida.

The State of Georgia has the White Cherokee Rose, *Rosa laevigata*, as its state flower. It is really native to China, although for many years has been naturalized in the southern states of North America. In legend it is also associated with an Indian girl who magical 'little people' turned into a flower when she was captured by a hostile tribe. They gave her further protection by covering the stem with sharp prickles and, indeed, this particular rose has very bristly stems.

Other states that have adopted roses as their state flowers include North Dakota (the Wild Prairie Rose, *Rosa pratincola)*, and the District of Columbia (the American Beauty Rose). However, neither state uses these roses on their State Seal.

Literature, Song and Art

Nature has long been utilized as a source of inspiration for writers, lyricists and artists. It is, therefore, not surprising that roses appear so often in literature and fine art as well as in legend and folklore. The bud, full-blown flower and thorns of the rose have all been used as metaphors and motifs.

Literature and Song

Throughout time, the rose has been immortalized by countless poets. Thomas Moore, the Irish poet famed for his graceful lyrics set to traditional tunes, gives a translation of the Greek lyric poet Anacreon's version of the origin of the rose:

> *Then, then, in strange eventful hour,*
> *The earth produced an infant flower,*
> *Which sprung with blushing tinctures drest,*
> *And wantoned o'er its parent's breast.*
> *The gods beheld this brilliant birth,*
> *And hailed the Rose, the boon of earth.*

Anacreon wrote chiefly in praise of love, food and wine. Ironically, he apparently died, at the age of eighty-five, choking on a grape pip.

Today, Thomas Moore is better known as the lyricist of 'Tis the Last Rose of Summer' which later received acclaim when featured in the opera *Martha* in 1847:

> *'Tis the last rose of summer,*
> *Left blooming alone;*
> *All her lovely companions,*
> *Are faded and gone.*

During the second century before the birth of Christ, Bion, a Greek pastoral poet from Smyrna and best known for his 'Lament of Adonis', suggested that all roses originally were white, later stained by the blood of Adonis or the amorous Venus.

The Roman poet Ausonius revealed in warm tones the beauty of new-blown roses in 'De Rosis Nascentibus', translated by the

The glory of summer roses is shown in Summer Offering by Sir Lawrence Alma-Tadema. The young girls hold lavish bouquets of pink and white roses.

English scholar Helen Waddell, an authority on medieval literature:

Think you, did Dawn steel colour from the roses,
Or was it new born day that stained the rose?
To each one dew, one crimson, and one morning,
To star and rose, their lady Venus one.
Mayhap one fragrance, but the sweet of Dawn
Drifts through the sky, and closer breathes the rose.

Shakespeare's enthusiasm for roses is clear, with numerous references to the flower in plays and sonnets. Perhaps the most often quoted reference to roses is Juliet's question in *Romeo and Juliet*:

What's in a name? that which we call a rose,
By any other name would smell as sweet.

A Midsummer Night's Dream abounds with references to roses, the bard having Oberon conjure up a bucolic scene:

Romeo and Juliet, the most famous lovers ever, are shown here in an illustration from Charles Folkard's and Alice Hofman's The Children's Shakespeare, published in 1911.

Henry Ryland (1856–1924) depicts a goddess holding pink roses in his painting, Purity. The delicate colours progress the idea of virtue and innocence in the picture.

I know a bank whereon the wild thyme blows,
Where oxlips and the nodding violet grows
Quite over-canopied with luscious woodbine,
With sweet musk-roses, and with eglantine:
There sleeps Titania some time of the night,
Lull'd in these flowers with dances and delight;
And there the snake throws her enamell'd skin,
Weed wide enough to wrap a fairy in.

with seasonal observations in Titania's, the Queen of Fairies, speech to Oberon:

Through this distemperature we see,
The seasons alter; hoary headed frosts,
Fall in the fresh lap of the crimson rose.

and the thoughts of Theseus on the fate of the unmarried Hermia:

But earthlier happy is the rose distill'd,
Than that which withering on the virgin thorn,
Grows, lives and dies, in single blessedness.

Robert Herrick, the seventeenth-century British Cavalier poet known for his pastoral and love lyrics, also compares roses to young, unmarried women in 'To Virgins, to Make Much of Time':

> *Gather ye rosebuds while ye may,*
> *Old Time is still a-flying;*
> *And this same flower that smiles to-day,*
> *To-morrow will be dying.*

This lyrical reflection on life was set to music and became one of the most popular songs of the seventeenth century.

Again in the seventeenth century, the English poet Edmund Waller, who in the Restoration period composed verse praising Charles II, wrote several popular love lyrics, including:

> *Go, lovely rose,*
> *Tell her, that wastes her time and me,*
> *That now she knows,*
> *When I resemble her to thee,*
> *How sweet and fair she seems to be.*

In the early nineteenth century, Thomas Hood, the English writer, wrote a ballad entitled 'It Was Not in the Winter' in which these lines feature:

> *It was not in the winter*
> *Our loving was cast!*
> *It was the time of roses,*
> *We plucked them as we passed!*

In 1855, William Makepeace Thackeray, probably most famously known for his novel *Vanity Fair*, wrote *The Rose and the Ring*, a humorous fairy tale. The plot involves the possession of a magic rose and a magic ring, which make the owner appear beautiful. One of the main characters is the maid Betsinda who is actually a princess by the name of Rosalba.

This beautiful painting, also by Henry Ryland, shows a pensive woman next to climbing pink roses. Falling petals lie by her feet.

Scottish literature is rich, none richer than in Robert Burns who wrote:

> *O, my Luve's like a red red rose*
> *That's newly sprung in June:*
> *O my Luve's like the melodie*
> *That's sweetly play'd in tune.*

In 'Ye Banks and Braie o' Bonny Doon' he wrote the lament:

> *And my fause lover stole my rose,*
> *But ah! he left the thorn wi' me.*

29

In this Flemish manuscript, circa 1500, The Poet or Dreamer in 'Roman de la Rose' finds his rose. In this allegory, the rose is a symbol for a lovely maiden.

French literature abounds with the delights of roses. The famous French poem 'Le Roman de la Rose' ('The Romance of the Rose') is an elaborate allegory on love and secular life. Begun in the latter half of the thirteenth century by Guillaume de Lorris, it was continued in the early part of the fourteenth century by Jean de Meung. During the later part of that century, Geoffrey Chaucer, poet and the father of English literature, translated 'Le Roman de la Rose,' part of which still exists and is called 'Romaunt of the Rose'.

The plot of the poem tells of a poet, called The Dreamer, being conducted by Dame Idleness into the Palace of Pleasure where he meets Love. Time is spent singing and dancing before he is led to a bed of roses. He selects one rose and attempts to pluck it, but is prevented.

Another French poem is 'Le Roi des Rimes' by the nineteenth-century dramatist and poet, Théodore de Banville. Study is compared with pleasure in the lines:

To study well the cons and pros
Should be our duty, I suppose . . .
Only words. Let's pick a rose.

While Jacques de Cassaigne reveals the feelings of a soldier addressing a rose:

One day you will die: but perhaps
I will die sooner than you,
For the death that my soul so fears,
May come at any time.
You will take a day to die,
I may only take a moment.

Gertrude Stein, the American poet, novelist and critic, subject of wide literary controversy in the 1920s, is characterized for her use of words for their associations and sounds rather than their literal meaning. Her much-quoted line, taken from 'Sacred Emily' –

A rose is a rose is a rose is a rose

– became famous, perhaps harkening back to Juliet's line in *Romeo and Juliet* or perhaps undressing roses of their glamour and legend and reminding the world that a rose is just a flower.

Few lyrics are so poignant as F. E. Weatherly's words to Haydn Wood's music for 'The Roses are Flowering in Picardy'. Initially popular during the later years of the First World War (it was published in 1916), for subsequent generations it became a sad reminder of comrades, relatives and friends lost in the terrible battles in northern France.

Roses are shining in Picardy,
In the hush of the silver dew.
Roses are flowering in Picardy,
But there's never a rose like you.
And the roses will die with the summertime,
And our roads may be far apart.
But there's one rose that dies not in Picardy.
'Tis the rose that I keep in my heart.

Other popular songs with a rose theme are 'Moonlight and Roses', 'Rose of Tralee', 'Mexicali Rose', and 'One Dozen Roses'.

Many poets and writers have contrasted life with the seemingly idyllic nature and aura cast by roses, none more amusingly than the Scottish novelist, poet and essayist Robert Louis Stevenson. In an essay, 'Virginibus Puerisque', in 1881, soon after returning from America where – after pursuing her from France – he had married Mrs Fanny Osbourne, he suggests:

Marriage is like life in this – that it is a field of battle, and not a bed of roses.

Architecture and Fine Art

One of the glories of medieval English architecture in churches has been rose windows, and especially those in York Minster, Exeter and Gloucester Cathedrals. The cathedral at Reims in north-east France also has a world-famous rose window.

This type of window was probably introduced by returning Crusaders who had admired the use of the rose in Islamic art. In addition to windows, rose motifs were used to embellish medieval tapestries and manuscript illustrations.

The rose was a popular northern European theme in medieval paintings depicting the Madonna. The Madonna was often situated in a rose garden or rose bower; the roses symbolizing her purity and virginity.

Roses have been depicted in paintings by many later artists, especially the Pre-Raphaelite Brotherhood, who used the rose as a romantic element. This group of artists united in about 1850 to resist existing conventions in art and literature by returning to art forms, as they believed them to be, before the time of Raphael, the Italian artist (1483–1520). They were strongly inspired by history, literature, nature and the Bible.

Other artists, such as Pierre-Joseph Redouté and G. D. Ehret were renowned for their artistic and botanically accurate studies of the rose.

Rose motifs are frequently used in decorative items. This tapestry cushion cover, from the sixteenth century, is linen embroidered with a silk and wool rose design.

Madonna of the Rose Bower, by Martin Schongauer, from the fifteenth century. Picturing the Madonna surrounded by roses was a popular theme for medieval artists.

The Language of Roses

AUSTRIAN ROSE (*Rosa foetida*)	Thou art all that is lovely
BURGUNDY ROSE (*Rosa centifolia*)	Simplicity and beauty; unconscious beauty
CABBAGE ROSE (*Rosa centifolia*)	Ambassador of love
CAROLINA ROSE (*Rosa carolina*)	Love is dangerous
CHINA ROSE (*Rosa chinensis*)	Grace or beauty ever fresh; beauty is always new
CLUSTER OF MUSK ROSES (*Rosa moschata*)	Charming
CROWN OF ROSES	Reward of virtue
DAMASK ROSE (*Rosa damascena*)	Brilliant complexion; beauty ever new
DOG ROSE (*Rosa canina*)	Pleasure mixed with pain; simplicity
FADED ROSE	Beauty, if fleeting
FULL-BLOWN ROSE PLACED **OVER TWO BUDS**	Secrecy
HUNDRED-LEAVED ROSE	Pride; the graces
'MAIDEN'S BLUSH' **ROSE** (derived from *Rosa alba*)	If you love me, you will find it out
MOSS ROSE (*Rosa centifolia*)	Voluptuous love; confession of love; superior merit
MOSS ROSEBUD	Confession of love

Lovers have always found ways, silently yet successfully, to pass messages to the temptations of their hearts. Encouraging smiles and winks are time-honoured lures, but saying it with roses is even more romantic. It is not even necessary to invest in large and perhaps expensive bouquets – just a single red rose will say it all.

Secret meanings have long been associated with plants in many countries and civilizations, but it was in the Orient that individual flowers came to acquire individual and precise meanings. In 1716, Lady Mary Wortley Montagu accompanied her husband to the Turkish court in Constantinople when he was appointed ambassador to the Porte, the Turkish name of the Ottoman court and government. From Pera (an area across the Golden Horn from St Sophia and now called Beyoglu) she sent a Turkish love letter to England, interpreting the meanings

This lovely pink rose is from an illustration in The Language of Flowers, a popular book during the Victorian times.

A Viennese Cafe, by Johann Hamza, shows a single rose being used to woo a woman. This popular custom is still prevalent today.

The spontaneity of courtship and flirtation is depicted in this painting, entitled Courtship, by Eugene de Blaas (1843–1931).

MULTIFLORA ROSE (*Rosa multiflora*)	Grace
MUSK ROSE (*Rosa moschata*)	Capricious beauty
PROVENCE ROSE (*Rosa centifolia*)	My heart is in flames
RED ROSEBUD	Pure and lovely; you are young and beautiful
'ROSA MUNDI' (*Rosa gallica* 'Versicolor')	Variety
ROSE IN A BRIDAL BOUQUET	Happy love
ROSE IN A TUFT OF GRASS	There is everything to be gained by good company
ROSE LEAF	I am never importunate
SINGLE ROSE	Simplicity
WHITE AND RED ROSES TOGETHER	Unity; warmth of heart
WHITE ROSE	I am worthy of you; silence
WHITE ROSEBUD	Too young to love; girlhood; a heart ignorant of love
WHITE ROSE FULL OF BUDS	Secrecy
WITHERED WHITE ROSE	Transient impressions
WREATH OF ROSES	Beauty and virtue rewarded
YELLOW ROSE	Infidelity; decrease of love; jealousy
YELLOW SWEETBRIAR	Decrease of love
YORK AND LANCASTER ROSE (*Rosa damascena* 'Versicolor')	War

of some plants, flowers and spices. The wonder of flowers, she claimed, was that words and messages of love could be passed in a refined manner, and even altercations could be conducted without the problem of getting ink on the fingers.

Lady Montagu was a celebrated letter-writer and society poet who later quarrelled with her close friend, the poet and satirist Alexander Pope.

The passing of messages through flowers was taken up by the French and later returned to England, early in the reign of Queen Victoria. Many books were then published, most taken from *Le Langage des Fleurs* by Madame de la Tour, although some lusty and forthright definitions had to be tempered to suit English tastes.

Although the language of flowers reached its height as a popular courtship custom in the nineteenth century, many of the meanings are still pertinent today. It is not only the rose itself that expresses a message, its presentation and positioning also means a great deal. For instance, a flower bent towards the right signifies 'I', while one inclined to the left means 'You'. Therefore, a red rosebud bent toward the left means 'you are pure and lovely'.

Leaves signify hope, and the thorns danger. So, a rose with leaves but with the thorns removed implies 'hopeful love and confidence'. When the flower is reversed, the meaning is also reversed.

The meaning of the flower is different depending on the hand – left or right – giving it. Similarly, the hand used to receive the flower relates a message. For instance, an affirmative is indicated by the right hand and a negative by the left. Thus, a Provence Rose, offered by the right hand, firmly confirms the sentiment 'my heart is in flames.' If taken by the right hand it would be sure to bring a smile to the giver!

The positioning of the flower on a woman's dress once had an important meaning: if placed over her heart, this clearly implied love, if in her hair it implied caution, while if set in her cleavage it meant friendship or remembrance. Particular flowers also created messages while in these positions, thus creating an extensive language.

Ribbons and the positions of knots also played a part in this elaborate love language. When viewed from the front, bouquets tied with knots on the left imparted a message from the giver. Knots on the right of the bouquet imparted messages about the recipient.

There are, of course, many other flowers which carry specific meanings, and by combining them in bouquets complicated and descriptive messages can be passed. For instance, 'You are beautiful, you are haughty, and I declare against you' is implied by a mixture of Japanese rose, purple larkspur and tansy (turned left when presented).

Although nowadays more direct and obvious ways are employed to woo a prospective partner – rather, in literary terms, like a book without a preface – using the beauty of flowers to impart a message does have merits. Cynics may observe that few people – even in Victorian times – ever read the preface to a book.

**THE MOSS ROSE –
LOVE VOLUPTUOUSNESS**

*The angel of the flowers, one day,
    beneath a Rose-tree sleeping lay;
Awakening from his light repose,
    the angel whispered to the Rose,
"O fondest object of my care,
    still fairest found, where all is fair;
For the sweet shade thou giv'st to me,
    ask what thou wilt, 'tis granted thee!"*

*"Then", said the rose, with deepened glow,
    "on me another grace bestow."
The spirit paused in silent thought: –
What grace was there the flower had not?
'Twas but a moment – o'er the Rose a
veil of moss the angel throws;
And robed in nature's simplest weed, could
there be a flower that Rose succeed?*

More so than any other hardy garden shrub, roses have captured the attention of flower lovers, for garden decoration and for displaying indoors in floral arrangements. Native roses are confined to temperate parts of the northern hemisphere, with only three or four species found in mountainous regions below the Tropic of Cancer. The native roses from these areas have been used to develop the modern roses we enjoy today.

The Development of Modern
—— Roses ——

In medieval England, the main roses grown were *Rosa alba, Rosa damascena,* the Damask Rose, and *Rosa gallica* – known as the French Rose and especially the Provins Rose, from its wide cultivation around Provins in the department of Seine-et-Marne to the southeast of Paris.

'Rosa Mundi' by the botanist G.D. Ehret (1710-1770). This well-known rose is Rosa gallica 'Versicolor'.

These medieval roses were very different from modern versions of the same plants. They had smaller flowers with gentler fragrances. However, some roses, such as the Apothecary's Rose (*Rosa gallica* 'Officinalis'), emitted an especially strong bouquet when it was dried.

Native to Europe and the British Isles are two other early roses: *Rosa phoenicia* and *Rosa canina,* the Dog Rose. Another early rose is the Autumn Musk Rose, *Rosa moschata.* As its name indicates, it is musk-scented and has creamy white single flowers during the late summer and into autumn. These roses are said to be the ancestors of the wealth of roses we know today. There were, of course, a few hybrids and sports that occurred, and these were included in the rose landscape.

During the years 1792 to 1824, four hybrid roses reached Europe from China and they introduced several desirable characteristics. These hybrids originated from *Rosa chinensis,* the China Rose (which introduced flower colours from pink to crimson), and *Rosa gigantea* (which introduced yellow flowers). It was a cross between *Rosa chinensis* and *Rosa gigantea* that produced *Rosa* × *odorata,* one of the parents of our modern Tea and Hybrid Tea Roses.

One of these four hybrid roses we know variously as 'Old Blush China', 'Parson's Pink China' or 'Monthly Rose'. It had been known in China for many centuries, having been illustrated in about 1000AD. Two of the others, 'Hume's Blush' and 'Parks' Yellow' appear to have been lost, but the fourth, 'Slater's

This pink rose was an early botanical drawing painted by Jacques Le Moyne de Morgues in the middle of the sixteenth century.

This botanical study is of the Rosa alba regalis, by Pierre-Joseph Redouté. This rose was commonly grown in medieval Europe.

North America has many superb native roses, such as *Rosa pratincola*, the Prairie or Climbing Rose, *Rosa virginiana*, and *Rosa stellata*, which comes from the State of New Mexico and is sometimes called the Gooseberry-leaved Rose.

As the development of modern roses continues, so does the quest for the hardiest and most perfectly formed rose. Hopefully the selection process will not result in any lost roses or in the forfeiture of beautiful scents and colours.

New Rose Classifications

New classifications of roses have been introduced to ease the complexity of so many types of roses. There are three main divisions.

Wild Roses encompasses roses which are natural species or varieties and hybrids which resemble species roses.

Old Garden Roses includes those which were widely grown before the origination of Hybrid Teas, both non-climbing and climbing forms, such as Alba, Bourbon, China, Damask, Gallica and Moss types as well as Noisettes and Climbing Teas.

Modern Roses covers roses which are neither Old Garden Roses nor Wild Roses. These are further arranged in non-climbing and climbing types, with the former housing, among others, the Hybrid Tea Roses, while the latter has Ramblers, Climbers and Miniature Climbers.

Species Roses

These are types that grow wild. The classification also includes their varieties and hybrids, which are man-made varieties created by crossing two species. A well-known example of a wild rose is *Rosa canina*, variously known as the Dog Rose, Briar (or Brier) Rose and Dog Brier, found in Europe, including Great Britain, and naturalized in North America. A spectacular variety of the

Crimson', is still grown, but for success needs a warm climate. Besides introducing new colours, these hybrids, although tender and not fully hardy, had a long-flowering nature, creating blooms throughout summer and until the frosts of autumn.

Later, during the 1800s, when hybridization was more fully understood, these roses provided a wonderful reservoir of scents, flower colours and long flowering periods that could be interwoven with earlier species to create a rich tapestry of varieties. There were, of course, other roses that played important parts in rose development, including the Species Roses *Rosa multiflora* and *Rosa pimpinellifolia*, also known as *Rosa spinosissima*, and commonly known as the Burnet Rose, Scots Briar or Scotch Rose. Central Asia also yields important native roses, such as the well-known *Rosa xanthina* and the gracefully ferny *Rosa webbiana*.

Dog Rose, which occurred by chance in a famous English garden, is 'Abbotswood'. Few could deny the beauty of its fragrant, fairly double, pink flowers borne in graceful, arching sprays.

The faintly fragrant *Rosa ecae* 'Helen Knight', raised in the Royal Horticultural Society's garden at Wisley, is an example of a man-made variety: the species is native to Afghanistan, but this particular variety was raised in cultivation in 1966 by Frank Knight, one of the directors of the society.

—— Old Roses ——

This class embraces a wide range of roses that arose as sports (mutants) or varieties from species mainly native to countries east of the Mediterranean and popular during the nineteenth century. Without exception they are very fragrant, and were widely grown before the introduction and popularization of Hybrid Tea Roses.

Rosa damascena from Les Roses by Redouté. Along with Rosa alba and Rosa gallica, this rose was frequently grown in medieval gardens.

ALBA types derived from *Rosa × alba*, variously known as the White Rose, White Rose of York and Jacobite Rose.

BOURBONS are descendants of *Rosa damascena* and *Rosa × odorata* and bear richly scented, cup- or globular-shaped blooms, densely packed with petals. They have a long flowering season, from midsummer to the frosts of autumn, and are borne amid dark, glossy green leaves.

DAMASKS have open and lax growth, originating from *Rosa damascena*. The leaves are downy and grey-green. Double, fragrant flowers are borne in loose clusters during midsummer. They produce long, slender hips in late summer.

This botanical work is of Rosa canina, the Dog Rose. It is a truly wild rose that is found native in Europe and Britain, and naturalized in North America.

The man-made Rosa ecae 'Helen Knight' was raised at the Royal Horticultural Society's garden at Wisley in 1966.

DWARF POLYANTHAS have mixed parentage: *Rosa multiflora* crossed with China Tea and Noisette types. They are small bushes, with many little pompom-shaped blooms, borne in large clusters mainly during midsummer, although they often flower again later.

GALLICAS are distantly removed from *Rosa gallica*. This is a large group, with dark green leaves and double, richly scented flowers, in colours from pink to crimson and mauve during midsummer. They are usually borne on stiff, upright stems.

HYBRID MUSKS, originating from *Rosa moschata*, the Autumn Musk Rose, have a lax, arching nature with leaves dark green above and grey-green below. During the latter part of summer and until the autumn frosts they bear scented flowers in a variety of colours.

HYBRID PERPETUALS owe their long flowering period to their Chinese parentage. They are hybrids of Bourbon and Portland Roses and were widely grown in Victorian times. Their popularity was usurped by the introduction of Hybrid Tea Roses. Their round and cabbage-like flowers are borne singly or in small clusters from midsummer to early autumn.

HYBRID RUGOSAS are results from crosses between *Rosa rugosa* and other rose species and hybrids. Their flowers, borne during midsummer and then sporadically until late summer, are usually heavily scented, initially bowl-shaped then opening flat.

HYBRID SWEETBRIARS, also known as Penzance Briars, were raised at the end of the nineteenth century. They are free-flowering, with richly scented, saucer-shaped, semi-double flowers in small clusters during midsummer.

MOSS ROSES are derived from *Rosa centifolia*, its sports and hybrids. They are associated with the Provence or Cabbage Roses, but differ in having the edges and backs of the sepals (the outer layer around a flower) covered with resinous, scented glands. Also, the flower stems are thickly covered with bristles. The double or semi-double flowers are borne during midsummer.

PORTLAND ROSES have *Rosa chinensis* – the China Rose and also known as *Rosa indica* – in their parentage and are the predecessors of the Bourbons and Hybrid Perpetuals. The Damask-type flowers appear during midsummer and intermittently through to autumn.

PROVENCE OR CABBAGE ROSES are derived from *Rosa centifolia* and bear fragrant, double flowers during midsummer.

SCOTCH ROSES owe their parentage to *Rosa spinosissima*, the Scotch or Burnet Rose, also known as *Rosa pimpinellifolia*. They are vigorous and suckering types, bearing fragrant, saucer-shaped flowers during the first half of the summer.

—— Modern Shrub Roses ——

These are hybrids between the Old Roses and Species Roses. They are variable, with single or semi-double flowers, which are flat when open. Flowering is mainly from mid to late summer, either singly or in small clusters. In attempting to produce a repeat-flowering rose bush many desirable characteristics have been lost in some progeny. However, a few of these hybridizations, such as the popular 'Constance Spry', have proved very successful.

—— Climbers and Ramblers ——

Important to all gardens for covering walls as well as pergolas and pillars, these two well-known types of roses have different growth styles. Climbers have stiff stems and smaller flower trusses than Ramblers, and a framework of mature stems. They bear flowers mainly on the current season's growth.

Ramblers, however, have long, vigorous, pliable stems. They bear flowers mainly on new shoots.

—— Hybrid Teas ——

The Hybrid Teas are now correctly known as Large-flowered Bush Roses. In 1971 the World Federation of Rose Societies accepted the British proposals that the name should be changed, so that Hybrid Tea Roses could be better described. However, such is the entrenchment and general acceptance of the old name that many rose nurseries still use the earlier terminology.

Hybrid Tea Roses – and no apologies are made for using the old, well-known name – are the successors to Hybrid Perpetuals. They create colour from mid to late summer with their large, usually double, bowl-shaped flowers. Hybrid Teas are the roses widely planted in rose beds. They are also much less bushy plants than their predecessors and breeding has often concentrated on attaining large flowers, long flowering seasons and new colours, sometimes at the expense of scent and grace.

Floribunda
—— Roses ——

This group has also been renamed as Cluster-flowered Bush Roses. Again, this was an attempt to provide a more precise description, but has not been widely taken up. They are derived from crosses between early Hybrid Tea Roses and Dwarf Polyantha types. Their arrival is relatively new.

In the early 1920s the Danish hybridist Svend Poulsen experimented to produce a rose with large flower trusses throughout summer. This he successfully accomplished in 1924 with 'Else Poulsen', followed by others, but it was not until 1952 that the term 'Floribunda' was accepted into rose terminology. Although these roses are said to lack the beauty and size of Hybrid Teas, they do flower throughout summer and into autumn. Recently introduced Floribundas, however, have been given qualities such as richer fragrance and increased flower size, which make it difficult to distinguish a Floribunda from a Hybrid Tea.

Some Floribundas are vigorous growers, while others are dwarfs. These dwarf types are often known as patio roses because they are suitable for planting around patios or at the front of borders.

—— Miniature Roses ——

These tiny bushes are both delightful and fascinating. Dainty and delicate semi-double or double flowers appear amid almost thornless stems during the first half of the summer. They often repeat flowering. Although true Miniatures are derived from *Rosa chinensis* 'Minima', cross-breeding has resulted in many Miniatures with Hybrid Tea and Floribunda attributes.

Red has long been the favourite colour for roses. This flower displays a stunning rich red colour and an exquisite form.

A Bouquet of Roses

ew flowers are quite as versatile as the rose. The rose provides colour and delight outdoors all through the summer and makes a superb cut flower, too. Its fragrance and form alone would make it a favourite to fill vases and bowls but it also offers a range of colours surpassing nearly every other florist's flower.

The magical scent of the rose has meant that it has always been in demand to make perfumes, and because this scent remains when the petals have been dried they have always made the most desirable pot-pourris and sweet bags. For centuries the rose has been cultivated commercially to produce the enticing oil of rose for perfumes, and distilled rose water is to this day a well-loved ingredient for many Middle Eastern recipes which demand the sweet scent and subtle flavour of the flower.

If you have a garden, then even just a few rose bushes will provide you with enough stems for arrangements, dried petals for pot-pourri and rose hips for cooking. Cutting off the fading flowers will keep the bushes flowering longer. If you cut the blooms before the end of the season, you can turn them into a fragrant home-grown pot-pourri. Rose flowers just opening out from the bud stage can be hung upside down in a warm, dry place and left to dry. They retain their colour very well and can be used to make lovely winter flower arrangements, either alone or mixed with other flowers.

Fresh roses look superb on their own, either as a generous bowlful or as a few stems in a narrow vase, but they also mingle very happily with many other types of flower

A flower-covered pitcher holds a mass of garden roses in many shades of red, crimson and pink all framed in a rustic cottage window.

and foliage to make little posies or extravagant arrangements on a large scale. Garden roses, unlike their shop-bought cousins, invariably come with short stems, so they are best crammed into a jug or low bowl. Their many-petalled heads and crumpled silky textures give a tapestry of colour and movement quite unlike any other flower.

There are very few guidelines needed for preparing and arranging roses except that it is always wise to re-cut stems at a sloping angle and hammer or split them a little way up if they are woody. Thorns are best removed and so are lower leaves – or all the leaves if you prefer – to prevent them tainting the water. Roses will always relish a long cool drink overnight or for several hours before they are put into an arrangement.

The brimming jugful of fresh garden roses, opposite, makes a vivid pool of colour in an old cottage window. During the peak of the season, make the most of these old-fashioned garden roses while they are available to pick. The short stems make them well-suited for a packed display in a complementary jug. The rose has always been a popular floral motif, providing inspiration for fabrics and china. The Victorian rose-covered quilt makes a perfect background to the boldly shaped jug decorated with strongly contrasting pink, cerise and scarlet blooms against the porcelain.

In the following pages there are dozens of ideas for using roses in a creative way. Whether you want to make a splendid arrangement, a delicious dessert, or a fragrant pot-pourri, the inspiration is here – in a bouquet of roses.

Beautiful red and pink roses growing in summertime are irresistible to pick. They can be used in pot-pourri and food as well as in sumptuous arrangements.

41

There is nothing more attractive than an arrangement of freshly cut roses during the height of the summer season. Since roses at this time of year are so luxurious and beautiful on their own, they often look best displayed simply. Baskets, jugs and low bowls as well as traditional vases can be used in a great variety of ways depending on the effect you want to accomplish. Use the following ideas as guides to create your own arrangement, or imitate them for practice.

—— A Basket of Roses ——

The rose more than any other flower has been an inspiration to artists from every time period. The nineteenth century artist, Fantin-Latour, was known for creating intimacy and repose in his still-lifes of flowers. Here, full-blown early summer roses capture the look of a Fantin-Latour painting. The many-petalled, heavy-headed blooms are richly perfumed and softly coloured, and anything else with them would spoil their perfection.

To achieve this kind of effect, line a basket carefully to make it waterproof and pack it with damp florist's foam. To make the roses last well, prepare all the roses by cutting the stems at an angle, removing lower leaves and thorns, and giving them a long drink before inserting them in the foam.

Most varieties in the rustic basket are old-fashioned roses such as 'Baron Girod L'Ain', 'Céleste', 'Gloire de Dijon', *Rosa gallica* 'Officinalis', and 'Fantin Latour', but some are quite modern roses bred to look similar in colour and form, and with the same wonderful scent as the old shrub roses. 'Aloha' is one of these, and another is the Floribunda 'Magenta'. Use complementing or contrasting shades of roses. The pinks, apricots and creamy whites used here make a subtle collection of roses.

A selection of old-fashioned roses are collected here in a rustic basket. Wherever this arrangement is placed, it will add a touch of the country garden.

Yellow Roses in
—— a Lustre Bowl ——

A shallow round bowl has been a traditional container for cut roses for many years. At one time a silver rose bowl was considered the perfect wedding present or anniversary gift, usually with a wire grille across the top to hold the flowers in place. A bowl like this does show off the large heads of Hybrid Tea Roses well if it is placed quite low on a piece of furniture, to allow it to be seen slightly from above.

This pretty pink-sponged lustre bowl with a gilt base is ideal for the rich mix of roses it contains. A mixture of golden yellow, blush pink and deepest apricot, the roses sit nestled in a cloud of acid green *alchemilla mollis* (lady's mantle) flowers. To support the heavy flowers it is necessary to use a block of florist's foam or crumpled wire netting in the bowl so that each bloom can be placed precisely where it is wanted.

Sweet Peas, Lavender
—— and Roses ——

Using a single colour of rose in an arrangement can often demand a contrasting shape, texture or colour to set the flowers off to their best advantage. Here roses of a rich buttery cream have been combined with soft lavender-coloured sweet peas and stems of fragrant French lavender. This gentle mix has been put into an exuberant and very colourful jug with an embossed pattern of twining rose branches. The simplicity of the flowers and their easy colours turn what could have been a daring idea into a lovely summer bouquet.

The narrow-necked jug does not need any extra support for the flowers unless the stems are very short; then a little crumpled wire would help. The roses are put in place first, then the sweet peas and lavender stems are simply tucked in between the large blooms where there is space.

Palest creamy yellow rose blooms are mixed with scented lavender and sweet peas to make an unusual colour combination which works beautifully in an exotic jug.

A richly lustred shallow bowl edged with gold makes the perfect container for buttery yellow, many-petalled roses offset by acid green alchemilla mollis flowers.

Red Roses and Blue Checks

Floribunda Roses, with clusters of flowers instead of a single or a few blooms on each stem, make excellent cut flowers if you are happy to sacrifice the colour from the garden. Most of the roses grown commercially and sold in flower shops are the long-stemmed single blooms which make good buttonholes (boutonnieres) and fit into formal arrangements but which lack the generosity of colour and texture which the multi-headed varieties have. However, there are some enlightened growers who are now providing the floristry trade with new rose varieties, which have multi-headed clusters similar to the garden Floribundas. Many of the new types are the result of crossing modern Floribundas with Hybrid Teas. Garden roses always seem to win hands down, though, when it comes to fragrance, with the old-fashioned varieties at the top of the league.

Brilliant scarlet might seem a difficult colour to work with but it is quite easy when you see that it simply demands strong colour and simple bold shapes to set it off well. Two types of brilliant red Floribunda Roses have been packed quite tightly into an old enamel French coffee pot. The crisp blue and white check design complements the velvety red petals perfectly. Only a very few green leaves have been left on the rose stems so as to keep the colour as concentrated as possible. Nothing else is needed to add to the flowers or the strong idea would be diluted. An arrangement like this would be at home in an old-fashioned country cottage or a sleek new city apartment, as its simplicity is quite timeless.

This idea would be every bit as stunning using deep pink, golden yellow or rich orange roses. Such a solid mass of flower heads would look good in any jug or coffee pot or even, in a slight variation to the theme, a tea pot.

A strong contrasting
effect is created with
a bunch of bold red
Floribunda Roses
massed together in
a blue and white
French coffee pot.

48

These are two quite different rose ideas, but both have a historical feel to them. The mellow blue jug holds a bunch of mixed cottage garden flowers reminiscent of a Tudor nosegay, while the little formal tree in a pot reminds one of the topiary and clipped evergreen hedges and path edges of Restoration gardens. Neither is difficult to make if you have the right ingredients.

The muted colours and faded design on an antique mug blends perfectly with a garden posy of roses and clematis, love-in-a-mist, marjoram and hardy geranium.

—— A Cottage Posy ——

An old faded blue and cream eighteenth-century mug makes a perfect resting place for this pretty pink posy. This kind of miniature arrangement is most easily put together in the hand then simply stood into its container. Begin by collecting a good range of mixed flowers and foliage such as roses, clematis, love-in-a-mist seed heads (*Nigella damascena*) and hardy geraniums. Make a bunch in your hands, thoroughly mixing the different flowers as you go. Tie or wire the bunch together and cut the stems off neatly, but not too short, at the bottom. Then stand the posy in the water-filled mug.

—— A Rosebud Tree ——

For this potted arrangement, you will need to pack an old terracotta plant pot with florist's foam and then stick in a woody twig. Push a ball-shaped piece of damp foam on to the top of the twig and densely cover this with short sprigs of evergreen leaves such as box, myrtle or sarcococca. Then push short-stemmed apricot rosebuds among the leaves, spreading them evenly around the ball. Finish off by scattering earth over the foam in the pot to give a naturalistic effect. You could also add a ribbon bow round the pot for a more extravagant look, or change the proportion of flowers to leaves for a more flowery and luxurious effect. A good idea is to make a pair of these ornate trees and stand them on either side of a doorway for a very noticeable and stately display.

A miniature rose tree cleverly constructed from twigs, sprigs of evergreens and small apricot rose buds. The earthy terracotta plant pot makes an attractive contrast to the formal flower ball.

—— 'Blue Moon' Rose Basket ——

This unexpected combination of colours makes the prettiest summer basketful of roses and sweet peas. The two deliciously scented flowers together complement each other and for a few weeks during the summer it should be easy to find both subjects at their peak and ready to combine in all manner of arrangements.

Baskets always make very sympathetic containers for all kinds of flowers. If you use one as a container for fresh flowers you have a choice as to how to treat it. Either line the basket with plastic film or foil then stand blocks of damp florist's foam inside, or use the basket as a decorative cachepot and stand any waterproof container in it to hold the flowers. For a dense and full effect such as this the foam block is the easiest method of supporting the flowers.

The 'Blue Moon' roses, which are in reality a more subtle smoky mauve than blue, look superb combined with several shades of warm yellow and apricot. To reinforce the colouring of the mauve rose, sweet peas in a clearer lavender shade have been added generously throughout the arrangement. No foliage has been used at all, which keeps the colour contrasts at their most saturated and effective.

There is a wonderful choice of baskets to be bought for using as flower containers, either in natural colours or spray-painted like the one here. If you want a very particular colour of basket then it is a simple job to stain with ink or paint a pale untreated basket to the shade you require. This soft aquamarine is a good colour which works well with many colour combinations and with the different greens of foliage.

This arrangement is a marvellous evocation of the richness of summer colours. The scented mixture includes pale mauve sweet peas and roses in subtle shades of lavender, apricot and peach.

Pastel Bunches

A few special rose blooms at the beginning or end of the season, or a gift of just one or two from someone you care about, deserve very special treatment. They look pretty grouped together, with single blooms or little bunches isolated from each other. You can create this arrangement by standing the roses in several matching wine glasses or tumblers and then either making a row of them or randomly positioning them in a group. Little flowers arranged in this way invite you to bend down and smell their perfume, so place them where it is easy to do this.

If you use clear or translucent glass containers, you may find that the effect is enhanced with light shining through them from behind. A sunny window-sill makes a perfect location. Or line them along a plain shelf against an uncluttered background to throw their shapes into relief.

Cool Cream Roses in a Jug

The creamy white flowers of a rose such as 'Iceberg' have a freshness and simplicity that few other flowers can match. They demand a simple treatment, too, if they are to look their best, so a container which is restrained and unfussy will suit them well. If you have plenty of blooms to pick, then make a show-stopping display to enjoy for several days. Jugs are wonderful containers for roses because they support the heavy heads naturally without looking contrived and they add some height to the whole arrangement. The narrowness of the neck keeps the rather spindly stems in order and the handle adds shape and variety to the overall outline. Old-fashioned wash bowls and matching jugs make beautiful containers for roses. Once the jug is filled with blooms and is standing in the bowl, an instant and interesting still-life is created.

The coolest white for a hot summer day. 'Iceberg' roses tumble from a graceful plain white jug and bowl and combine successfully with the aqua blue of poppy seed heads.

Small roses and single flowers deserve special treatment. Display blooms in a cluster of little frosted tumblers to preserve their delicacy.

— Roses and Glass Vases —

Roses come in every shade of pink, from eye-catching shocking pink to delicate shell. Within each flower, because of the densely packed petals and play of light, there can be many shades of one colour. This is why it is always very successful to combine lots of different pink roses together. Many of the Old Rose varieties such as 'Comte de Chambord,' 'La Reine Victoria,' and 'Petite de Hollande' are a wonderful rich sugary pink like crushed raspberries and cream. Modern roses very often have more orange and yellow in the pink, and edge towards peach and salmon shades. A few newer varieties, though, have the rich old-fashioned pink colouring – such as the well-loved 'Constance Spry' or 'Pink Favourite' and the Climber 'Pink Perpetue'.

A dramatic display of pink roses all arranged in clear sparkling glass. Do not be afraid to mix all the pinks together to create a clashing mixture.

Glass makes a sparkling container for rose blooms and all kinds of shapes can be put to good use. You can use elaborate cut glass if you have it, or simple straight-sided modern tanks or cylinders. Small glass jars or dessert dishes are good for little posies and stemmed wine or liqueur glasses are wonderful ways to present exquisite single blooms or specimen flower heads. It is still possible to find antique pressed glass quite cheaply, and moulds and stands are useful to display low arrangements of massed rose flower heads.

Whichever type of glass container you choose, remember that the most important thing is that the glass is sparkling clean and the water inside as clear as possible. You will probably need to change the water frequently. Make sure that there are no rose leaves left on the stems under the water, as this will cause the water to turn green and cloudy. There are proprietary crystals available at florist's shops to put into the water to help keep it clear and fresh. A more old-fashioned trick is to put a small piece of charcoal at the bottom of the vase.

Rose Posies

Traditionally, rosebuds have always been used in posies. From the original tussie-mussies of the seventeenth century, which were carried at all times to keep plague and infectious diseases at bay, to the neatly organized Victorian bunches edged with white lace and inserted into ornate silver holders, the rose has taken a predominant place among flowers.

The early tussie-mussies were made up of a variety of medicinal herbs and may have included rosemary, lemon balm, rue, marjoram, and hyssop with just a few flowers of either rose, lavender, or wallflower. By Victorian times, flowers to include were often chosen according to the message that each type was supposed to convey; the rose has long signified 'love'. However, posies have many other uses besides the ones traditionally ascribed to them. They can be used for decorating tables or wrapped gifts, or for adorning hair, hats or attire. They are often used to form parts of garlands or wreaths.

Posies are put together in the hand, building up flower by flower. They can be arranged in a formal pattern with rings of one type of flower round a central bloom, or they can be simply a random mix of colours and sizes of blooms for a more natural and relaxed effect. Posies designed to be carried at a wedding are usually made by wiring the stems, which makes it easier to push each flower into the right place. A posy made as a gift for a friend can simply be put together without wire and then placed in a suitable container to be enjoyed for a while longer.

To make either of the posies pictured here, or one of your own invention, begin by cutting all stems to the same length. Start with one good bloom or a little bunch of flowers in the centre and add flowers and leaves around the edge, turning as you proceed to keep the arrangement even. A posy should never be so large that it is uncomfortable to hold in the hand, so stop if the bunch of stems is getting too thick. You can decorate the outer edge with a fringe of pretty foliage or make a paper doily frill to contain the posy and give it a romantic look. Finish by securing with wire or florist's tape and a complementary ribbon.

Traditionally the rose and rosebud have always been used for posies because of their neat habit and perfect shape. Here they are mixed with anemones and pale peach statice.

*Palest lemon
Miniature Roses are
mixed with cottage
garden astrantia,
lavender and
agapanthus and
completed with
ribbon and netting.
A perfect design for
a wedding posy.*

A Rose-Filled Wreath

Roses mix very happily with all kinds of summer flowers and one of the most stunning ways of showing them off is to combine them with a vibrant range of colours to echo the flower paintings and porcelain decoration of the eighteenth century.

Garlands and wreaths are not difficult to make if you have the right materials to make a base and a good choice of flowers. The traditional way to make a circular garland would be to build up a moss or straw form on which to put the flowers and then wire them into position. Kept damp and sprayed frequently, this type of garland wreath would

last for a few days. Now that we have florist's foam to keep flowers fresh it is possible to make wreaths very quickly by pushing short stems straight into the damp foam. You can buy rings of foam with solid plastic bases and these can be hung on a door or wall or the whole flower-covered ring can lay flat on a horizontal surface, such as a table.

Yet another option is to cut out any shape you want to cover with flowers from the flat sheets of foam which are available. In this way you can make a graceful oval shape like the one here, which is based on an old flower painting, complete with a flowing

Piles of summer flowers along with roses are gathered to be made into an extravagant oval wreath. You will need a damp foam base to create the shape and sharp scissors. The flowers will stay fresh for several days.

ribbon which has always been an important accessory for wreaths. Rich pink roses mingle with smaller pale pink rosebuds alongside many other old-fashioned flowers – pinks and scabious, lilies and cornflowers, sweet Williams and poppy seed heads. All the flowers are cut to roughly the same length so that when they are pushed into the foam the flowers make a smooth surface. It is important to cover any of the foam which might show, especially on the inside bottom edge. It is easiest to work systematically round the foam shape, as the effect should be quite random and informal.

The finished wreath is decorated with a sumptuous pale green velvet ribbon to give the arrangement an eighteenth century air.

Rosebud Garlands

In medieval times the most popular form of flower decoration was a garland or long chain of flowers, often limited to a red, white and green colour scheme. Wealthy women would spend many hours in groups creating long swags to decorate churches for feast days or their homes for celebrations and special occasions. Nowadays this form of flower arranging is usually limited to weddings or Christmas decorations but lingers on in the daisy chains which children still make in summertime. A long rope of flowers has also come back into fashion to be carried by a bride's attendants, and this makes a pretty alternative to posies or flower-filled baskets. Use a long swag of roses to adorn a plain wall or to twine through banisters or up pillars. A soft tasselled rope will make a good base on which to wire the roses as it bends easily and achieves a curved outline. Also, a garland of rosebuds makes the prettiest edging to a buffet table, where it can be pinned round the top edge or looped and caught with small bunches of the same flowers or contrasting posies.

By their nature garlands are short-lived and designed to look pretty only for the length of the special event. Some flowers will remain fresh out of water longer than others, and roses survive very well as each flower head has body and substance which keeps it in shape for several hours. You can wire your flowers on to a length of soft rope or cord or work straight on to wire.

For the pale pink rosebud garland pictured here, individual buds have been wired along a length of wire alternating with bunches of tiny Miniature Roses. Little posies pinned on to the gauzy white cloth hold the garland in place. If you want more greenery among the flowers and a more solid effect, then blooms can be wired on to lengths of evergreen smilax (*Asparagus medeoloides*). The smilax plant is sold in long swags and is trained to grow up a trellis tied with threads just for this commercial purpose.

Garlands and ropes of roses have been made since Roman times. Here a swag of pale pink rose buds and little posies decorates a table for a midsummer buffet party.

The roses and rosebuds of the Hybrid Tea 'Lady Sylvia' are beautifully formed and ideal for creating a delicate pink garland.

A Pot-Pourri of Roses

In Elizabethan times every well-run house-hold would gather or buy large quantities of sweetly scented rose petals in the summer to dry for use throughout the rest of the year. These petals were powdered and mixed with fixatives and spices to create deliciously scented concoctions to fill small bags or bowls used to scent and freshen linen and stored clothes, or to sweeten the air in a musty room.

Later, by the eighteenth century, true pot-pourris were being made, designed to be kept in little lidded jars. The pot-pourri jar would be warmed in front of a fire when needed, then the lid lifted to scent the room with a cleansing floral and spicy fragrance. The most important flower ingredient for pot-pourris was the rose which kept its frag-rance so well and was widespread and abundant. Other flowers which were often included were lavender, pinks, jasmine and garden violets.

Moist Pot-Pourris

The original method made a moist pot-pourri, for which semi-dried petals and leaves were layered with salt and when ready mixed with further herbs, spices and fix-atives. The vital ingredients include rose petals, coarse non-iodized salt and fixative. Although it may take all summer to make a moist pot-pourri, the result will be more long-lasting and authentic than shop-bought pot-pourris, which are usually only scented with essential oils and a little fixative. Essen-tial rose oil may be used to reinforce the natural scent of the rose or to boost the fragrance after it has faded.

The basic ingredients for a traditional moist pot-pourri are semi-dried rose petals and coarse salt. 'Rosa Mundi' and Rosa gallica 'Officinalis' are exceptionally scented and a recommended choice for pot-pourri.

Collect fresh rose petals on a dry day and spread them out on frames to dry. An idea for a summer wedding is to pick baskets of rose petals for guests to use as natural confetti.

To partially dry rose petals, place them on a tray or fine-meshed frame in a warm cupboard or attic until they are leathery. They may blow away if placed outside in the sun. The moist version is beautifully scented but does not have a naturally good colour and needs to be decorated with dried flowers or whole spices to make it look attractive if it is displayed in an open bowl. However, many other containers can be used to display the textures and colours of pot-pourri – pottery bowls, ceramic or china dishes, or even antique tin or wooden boxes. Baskets make particularly lovely containers, but they may need to be lined with fabric so the pot-pourri does not seep out. For special effect, insert whole dried rose heads into the basket rim. For a moist pot-pourri recipe see page 66.

Moist pot-pourris need the addition of brightly coloured dried flower heads to enliven their otherwise dull colour.

Here is a rose pot-pourri made from pink and red rose buds, cornflower petals and larkspur. Choose a bowl which suits the scale of the mixture and enhances its colour.

—— Dry Pot-Pourris ——

Nowadays we mostly make a dry type of pot-pourri, which involves drying flower petals fully and mixing with other dried leaves and flower heads. Spices, both whole and ground, are added, and a fixative holds the scent. A dry pot-pourri needs the addition of essential flower oils to boost the scent which is not otherwise as strong as it is in a moist version. The advantage of a dry pot-pourri is that it holds its colours and looks very pretty to display in open containers.

The wonderful thing about making your own pot-pourris is that you can experiment with colours and scents as you choose. A good basic recipe can be adapted to suit you and your materials, but try this rose recipe first and then be creative with your own ideas. This recipe makes a deep red and pink pot-pourri. You might like to add more contrast by mixing in some green, using either dried lemon verbena leaves or crumbled dried bay leaves. If the fragrance fades after a while, simply refresh it with a few more drops of rose essential oil.

4 cups of dried rose petals, preferably red or deep pink as these usually have the strongest scent
1 cup whole pink or red dried rosebuds
1 cup dried lavender flowers
½ cup powdered orris root
1 tablespoon ground allspice
1 tablespoon ground cinnamon
1 tablespoon ground nutmeg
½ tablespoon ground cloves
Several drops of essential rose oil

The fixative used here, orris root, is the dried, powdered root of *Iris florentina* and is sold in natural health and craft shops. Another common fixative is gum benzoin.

Combine all the dry ingredients in a large bowl, sifting and mixing them well with your fingers. Add drops of essential oil judiciously until the scent is strong enough. Transfer into a paper bag and seal. Leave in a cool dark place for six weeks to cure, shaking it occasionally. Display it in shallow baskets or bowls and decorate the top with large dried rose blooms or little bundles of whole cinnamon sticks.

It is sensible to dry rose petals and store them in their separate colours, then they can be mixed with other ingredients and spices later to create unique pot-pourri recipes.

A Fragrant Moist Pot-Pourri

It is claimed that a well-made pot-pourri can retain its scent for very many years, and judging by old recipes obviously much time and care went into the preparation of them. If you have a garden and grow roses then you can make one over a number of weeks, adding fresh petals as they come along. The finished product will be basically brown and not very attractive but the scent is superb. Either keep it in a covered box or basket and just open it occasionally or put it in a perforated container. You can also arrange it in a dish or basket and decorate the top with prettier dried flowers, twists of citrus peel or whole pomanders.

This pot-pourri is made from roses only, but other scented flowers can be added with the spices. If you do this, these flowers should first be fully dried. Do use coarse, non-iodized salt.

10 cups partially dried rose petals
About 3 cups coarse salt
2 tablespoons ground cinnamon
2 tablespoons ground allspice
2 tablespoons ground nutmeg
1 tablespoon ground cloves
5 tablespoons powdered orris root
Few drops of essential rose oil

Use only highly scented, preferably red, rose petals. Partially dry them until leathery, then layer petals and salt in a large bowl. Weight down and stir every day, draining off any moisture. After three to six weeks, crumble the mixture and add spices and essential rose oil. Seal into paper bags and cure for about six weeks before using.

This moist pot-pourri is well-suited for scenting the bedroom. Although this type is not particularly decorative, it can be enhanced by placing a few dried whole roses on top.

Little linen bags are very quick and simple to make. Filled with rose pot-pourri, they give laundry a lovely scented freshness. They also make superb gifts.

—— Rose-Scented Sachets ——

Sachets are delightfully old-fashioned ideas which are still as popular as ever. Little muslin or fabric bags are filled with sweetly scented pot-pourri and used to tuck among shirts or underwear, sheets, towels and blankets or clothes stored away. The quickest and simplest bags to make are those which do not need any sewing. You can either cut squares or circles of thin cotton fabric or lawn, or use ready-made handkerchiefs. A scoop of pot-pourri is placed on the centre of the fabric and the whole thing simply gathered up and tied round the top with a piece of cord or ribbon. You can, if you like, pad out the bag with wadding to make a softer, fatter shape.

A pot-pourri mixture for a sachet or bag should not have too many ground spices which might be finely powdered and spill out of the bag; crushed spices are best, although you will need powdered orris root as usual as the fixative.

If you like sewing, then you can make up all kinds of shapes of sachet for specific purposes. A small sack is useful attached to a clothes hanger to put inside a wardrobe, and little flat discs slide easily between layers of delicate clothes in a drawer. Devise your own personal style of recipe based on what you have in the garden. This basic rose recipe is sweet and delicate and suits many purposes. Adapt it as you like, making it spicier or sharper as you choose.

1 cup sweetly scented, dried rose petals
½ cup lavender flowers
½ cup crushed lemon verbena leaves
½ cup crushed rosemary needles
2 crushed cinnamon sticks
¼ cup powdered orris root
Few drops of essential rose oil

Mix all the dry ingredients in a large bowl. Add drops of oil until you get the right strength of fragrance. Put the mixture in a paper bag, seal and leave in a dark cool place for about two weeks. Use to fill sachets and bags and, if you have some left over, fill a fabric-lined basket with the pot-pourri and stand it in a bedroom, laundry room, nursery or even a wardrobe to scent the air.

The crisp astringent fragrance of lavender combines perfectly with that of roses. Put pot-pourri in a small fabric-lined basket to stand in a bedroom or bathroom.

Roses of Luxury

Rose petal water has a mild and sweetly fragrant tonic effect on the skin. The summer is the best time to capture the fragrance of roses in a rose water you will use year round.

The rose has a long history of use as a means to more beautiful skin and hair. The irresistible fragrance makes it a popular choice for perfuming all kinds of beauty products from shampoo to hand cream. Rose water at one time was sprinkled on to clothes, hair, linen and even on to guests as they arrived at a house. It is doubtful you would want to do this today but home-made rose petal water is lovely to use as a mild skin toner and freshener or to sprinkle into a warm bath.

—— Rose Petal Water ——

Put five cups of fresh rose petals in a large bowl and over this pour boiling water (preferably spring water). Add vodka, or medicinal alcohol if you can buy it, in the proportion 1 part spirit to 10 parts water. Leave to infuse. When cool, strain into sterilized bottles and cork. Add a fresh petal or two to each bottle.

—— Rose Hand Cream ——

Use this soothing lotion to condition hands or feet, or whenever you get dry skin.

2 tablespoons fresh rose petals
4 tablespoons almond oil
8 tablespoons lanolin
4 tablespoons glycerine
Several drops of essential rose oil

Cover rose petals with a little boiling water and leave to cool. Gently melt the almond oil, lanolin and glycerine in a bowl over hot water. Put into a food processor and add well-drained rose petals and rose oil. Process until the petals are distributed throughout the mixture and all is well blended. Pour into small glass jars.

—— Bath Sachets ——

One of the most useful ways to add roses to your bath is to make small bath sachets of dried flowers and herbs which can be dropped into the hot water or tied to the tap while the water runs into the bath. Use muslin or cheesecloth to make the bags and add oatmeal or powdered milk to add softness to the water along with the fragrant and restorative powers of the flowers. Roses make perfect ingredients for bath sachets, with perhaps a little lavender or rosemary added for spice.

A rich and moisturizing cream can easily be made from natural ingredients with the addition of roses for rich scent and a soothing effect. Pot up into small glass jars and use regularly.

Scented Bath Oil

Bath oils and foams help to make a relaxing experience even more pleasurable. There is a wide selection of different kinds of oil on sale in shops but many are sadly disappointing, relying on artificial fragrances and lurid colours. Many of them actually dry the skin more than condition it.

To make a bath oil, simply mix 3 parts of glycerine with 1 part of essential rose oil and pour into a jar. When you bathe take out just a teaspoon or so and add as you are running the hot water. Soak for ten minutes or more and then when you are dry splash on rose petal water (see page 70).

A Rose Petal Facial

Another soothing use of roses is in a facial steam bath. This, if it is not too hot, refreshes and enlivens dull skin. The easiest way to make a facial steam bath is to pour boiling water into a large bowl and to add a handful or two of fresh rose petals. Then add a few drops of an essential rose oil – tea rose is particularly pleasant – and put your face over the bowl, draping your head with a towel to keep the steam in. Steam for about ten minutes or for as long as you desire. You can add different flowers or make a mixture using herbs. Finish off with a gentle splash of rose petal water to tone the skin.

A facial steam bath is a quick reviver for skin that has a tough time in city air and polluted atmospheres. Ten minutes can leave you feeling refreshed and your skin softened and cleaned.

A bath scented with roses is luxurious and relaxing. Roses have been used for centuries in beauty preparations and they still retain their popularity today.

Storecupboard Recipes

Roses have been popular culinary ingredients for centuries. As well as being renown for their medicinal attributes, they were relished for the flavour and scent they added to food.

The fruit of the wild rose has been gathered for centuries to make preserves, wine and syrups. Our ancestors sensibly made use of this free harvest and provided themselves with the most marvellous source of vitamin C without knowing it. Many garden rose varieties develop hips which can be used in the kitchen, and types such as the *Rugosa* roses bear enormous thick-fleshed hips which are easy to manage. The seeds must always be removed from the hips as they are sharp, prickly and unpalatable.

Here are two delicious recipes which will remind you of summer roses all through the year. They can be stored long-term in your pantry or kitchen cupboard.

—— Rose Hip Syrup ——

Rose hip syrup is a delightful old recipe worth reviving. Pour a little over desserts and ice creams or use to mix into drinks and fruit cups for colour and the combination of sweetness and sharpness.

To make rose hip syrup, follow this recipe. You may want to multiply the measurements to make a larger amount.

1 lb (2½ cups) ripe rose hips
1½ pint (about 4 cups) water
1 lb (2½ cups) granulated sugar

A richly glowing harvest of autumn fruits and rose hips made into syrups, chutneys and jams. Rose hips have a high vitamin C content and a fresh astringent taste.

Pick ripe rose hips, remove seeds, crush, and put into boiling water. Bring back to the boil and simmer for 20 minutes. Strain the liquid through muslin and put the strained juice back into the pan. Add the sugar and heat gently until the sugar has been dissolved. Remove mixture from the heat and pour into hot clean bottles or jars. Keep in a refrigerator.

To store for longer periods the bottles must be sterilized. Put the bottles in a deep pan, keeping them apart from each other and with their bases on a trivet. The water should be level with the bottlenecks. Tie down or fasten tops, then simmer for 20 minutes at 88°C (190°F). After sterilizing, tighten tops and leave to cool.

—— Rose Hip Autumn Chutney ——

Another delicious recipe using rose hips is a spicy chutney to eat with cold meats, cheese or Indian dishes. Collect the hips when they are fully ripe and beginning to soften and split each one to remove the seeds.

8 oz (2 cups, chopped) courgette (zucchini)
2 tablespoons salt
8 oz (2 cups) prepared rose hips
8 oz (2 cups) apples, peeled and chopped
8 oz (2 cups) ripe tomatoes, skinned and chopped
8 oz (2 cups) onions, peeled and chopped
4 oz (1 cup) sultanas (golden raisins)
4 cloves garlic, crushed
1 lb (3 cups) light brown sugar
¾ pint (2 cups) wine vinegar
1 teaspoon ground cinnamon
1 teaspoon ground allspice
½ teaspoon cayenne

Chop courgette (zucchini) into small pieces and sprinkle with the salt. Leave to drain for an hour. Rinse and dry and put in a large pan with all the other ingredients. Heat gently, stirring until the sugar dissolves. Cook gently until the chutney is thick and jam-like. Pot into hot, sterilized jars and seal well. Leave to mature for a few weeks before eating. Makes about 3lb.

Sweet Edible Delights

Rose petals give a delicious fragrance and flavour to all kinds of sweet treats. Recipes remain from Elizabethan times for rose petal jams and jellies, syrups and sweetmeats, and many of these translate very well to today's style of eating.

For rose-flavoured recipes always try to find triple-distilled rose water which is available from chemists (pharmacies) and food shops. This is the type suitable for food and has strong flavour and no additives.

—— Rose Petal Sorbet ——

Serves 6

For summer eating on warm days try a rose petal sorbet to refresh and cleanse the palate.

4 oz (¾ cup) caster (superfine) sugar
¾ pint (2 cups) water
Pared rind and juice of 2 well-scrubbed unwaxed lemons
About 1½ cups scented rose petals
2 teaspoons triple-distilled rose water
1 egg white

In a pan dissolve the sugar in the water. Add lemon rind. Bring to the boil and simmer for 6 minutes. Remove from heat, add the rose petals and leave to cool. Strain syrup and add lemon juice. Flavour further with rose water to taste. Freeze in a covered plastic container until mushy then whisk in stiffly beaten egg white. Freeze again until firm. Allow to soften slightly before serving in chilled glasses.

Delicate custard glasses hold scoops of soft and scented rose petal sorbet which makes a delicious end to a summer meal. Decorate with a geranium leaf and serve with crisp macaroons.

—— A Midsummer Rose Cake ——

At midsummer indulge in a celebratory party among the rose blooms. Cut out the centre of your favourite sponge cake and fill it with fresh strawberries, rose petal jam (see page 78) and cream. Cover the whole cake with more whipped cream and scatter toasted almonds or coconut strands over it. Decorate the cake with a few pink blooms from a single wild rose or Sweetbriar.

—— Rose Petal Decorations ——

During the rose season, crystallize some rose petals to store for decorating cakes and desserts through the winter. Dissolve powdered gum arabic in rose water and paint this on to each petal, then dip the petals into caster (superfine) sugar and lay on a grill or wire rack somewhere warm to dry and crispen. Store in an airtight container.

A midsummer birthday party demands the most glamorous cake, complete with cream, candles, strawberries and roses. Decorate the table with more rose sprays and enjoy a feast.

A Rose-Scented Tea Party

A traditional mid-afternoon tea is a great excuse to make sweet foods and a wonderful time to use roses. Along with jams and tarts, and of course tea itself, roses can also be used to add exquisite decoration to the table. Here are a few ideas for using roses for a special tea party.

Rose Petal Jam

Rose petal jam can be rather sweet and cloying so a better way to use rose petals in a preserve is to make a sharp-flavoured base from apples or redcurrants and then flavour with rose petals. Or try using the rose petals with other summer fruits such as a strawberry and rose jam or redcurrant, nectarine and rose petal conserve.

Rose Tea

For a feast of rose flavours make your own rose-scented tea to drink with all the sweet delights. To do this you will need some strongly scented, dried rose petals which you simply add to a high quality, large leaf, China tea such as Keemun. The proportions are rather up to your taste but begin by using 2 tablespoons of dried petals to 3½ oz (3½ cups) tea. Mix them together and store in an airtight tin. Prepare the tea in the usual way and serve it without milk or lemon.

Flavoured Sugar

Scented rose petals can be used to flavour sugar. Put 4 tablespoons of dried petals into 1lb (2½ cups) caster (superfine) sugar and store in a glass jar with a ground glass stopper. Use the sugar in custards, cream puddings, cakes, or to sweeten plain yoghurts.

Finish preparing for your rose tea party by decorating the table and food with fresh rose petals. Gather them from the garden and scatter over fruit tarts and desserts.

Roses to eat, drink and look at. Rose petal jam turns plain scones into a special treat and rose petal tea is a perfect refreshing drink to accompany such an extravagant spread of flowers and fruit.

A Glossary of Roses

The range of roses is wide and often bewildering. Their classifications are numerous and sometimes complex to novice rose enthusiasts. Most roses are grouped according to their parentage, while some are placed according to their nature, such as climbers, which are able to fill walls and screens with colour. It is, therefore, clear that some roses can be slotted into one or more groupings. For example, the Old Rose 'Madame Plantier' is claimed by both Alba and Noisette devotees, and can be grown as a shrub in a border or as a climbing rose. Early Miniature Roses once had an affinity to China Roses and were often known as *Rosa chinensis minima,* but now have complex parentages often associated with Hybrid Teas, Floribundas and Polyanthas.

Classifying roses, therefore, is in some regards an art and judgement, rather than a science. However, not attempting an overall classification results in chaos and, eventually, disenchantment. Additionally, creating a general view of the groupings, and then highlighting the deviants of these groupings creates further interest.

Hybrid Teas are thought by many rose enthusiasts to be the epitome of perfection. They are now known as Large-flowered Bush Roses. Floribundas have also had a name change – to Cluster-flowered Bush Roses. These new classifications for Hybrid Teas and Floribundas allow them to be arranged by their appearance and the way their flowers are formed rather than by parentage; with increased intermingling of parents, it is becoming nearly impossible to classify them by their ancestry. And what

This beautiful 'Raubritter' rose displays clusters of bright pink, cup-shaped blooms. It is well suited for forming a hummock near a bank.

primarily matters to home gardeners who grow roses is a plant's appearance, not its parentage, however interesting that may be to rose aficionados.

Roses that clamber and climb are an essential part of a garden, and most gardens have space to accommodate at least one of them. Pillars, pergolas and trellises are alternatives if wall space is not available. A further method is to allow a rose to wander through a tree, creating an exciting colour and tone harmony. If space is not present for Climbers, most gardens have room for Miniature Roses, either in beds alongside patios, in tubs or window-boxes.

Roses which have a rich historical legacy are the Species, as well as the Old Roses and Modern Shrub Roses. Exciting representatives of these groups are featured, many having vibrant flowers and attractive leaves, as well as colourful hips in autumn. These are also known as heps and are the seed pods of a rose.

With all of these roses an indication of heights are given, and also spread widths for some. The climate, soil fertility and, with some roses, the severity of pruning influences a plant's vigour, and therefore the figures can only be taken as a guide.

The number of new roses introduced each year by rose nurseries is immense and world-wide, and in part this accounts for the wide range of names some roses gather about themselves. Space has been available to reveal only a small proportion of the many new and exciting roses. However, it is not only new varieties that are worth growing, and many old and well-loved roses are featured in this glossary.

The strong scent and striking cream and red colours makes this Hybrid Tea, 'Double Delight', an outstanding rose.

Hybrid Tea Roses

These roses are now known as Large-flowered Bush Roses. They are thought by many rosarians to be aristocrats, the crème de la crème of the rose world, creating large and dominant flower heads intermittently from midsummer to the frosts of autumn. The exact time when the first flowers appear is strongly influenced by the latitude, and usually they are borne in flushes.

The colour range is remarkably wide and many are famed for their superb scents, while some are ideal for cutting and arranging in flower displays indoors.

'Alec's Red'

'Alec's Red'
Height: 90cm–1m (3–3.5ft)
Spread: 90cm (3ft)
This is said to be the best red rose. Introduced in 1972 from a cross between 'Fragrant Cloud' and 'Dame de Coeur', it has won many prizes. Other roses in its parentage are 'Peace' and 'Independence'. It has large, full-petalled, globular, cherry-red flowers on plants with a strong, upright stance. Its fragrance is sweet and strong.

It has the benefit of dark, glossy foliage, with flowers borne on strong leaf stalks. Additionally, the blooms are resistant to rain and retain their colour as they age. It is also resistant to disease.

'Alexander'
Height: 1.2m (4ft)
Spread: 90–100cm (3–3.5ft)
Also known as 'Alexandra', this 1975 introduction has 'Ann Elizabeth' 'Allgold' and 'Super Star' in its parentage. It creates a tall, robust, vigorous and free-flowering plant. It bears medium-sized, brilliant orange-

vermilion, slightly fragrant flowers. The foliage is semi-glossy and dark green, and the whole plant is resistant to diseases. It is ideal for planting as a hedge or for positioning in a large rose bed. Because of their long stalks, the flowers are ideal as cut flowers.

'Alexander'

'Bettina'
Height: 75–90cm (2.5–3ft)
Spread: 75–90cm (2.5–3ft)
Derived in France from a crossing between 'Peace' and a progeny derived from 'Madame Joseph Perraud' and 'Demain', this Hybrid Tea was introduced in 1953. It has distinctive blooms, orange with a golden base, heavily veined, and flushed salmon and red. The slightly fragrant flowers are borne on vigorous but branching plants, with glossy, bronze-tinted foliage. It is susceptible to black spot disease and best avoided if your location is damp. However, the blooms are resistant to rain and are superb as cut flowers.

'Bettina'

'Big Chief'

'Blessings'

'Blue Moon'

'Big Chief'

Height: 1–1.2m (3.5–4ft)
Spread: 90cm (3ft)
Introduced in 1975 from a cross between 'Ernest H. Morse' and 'Red Planet', this rose has been acclaimed by many rosarians. Sometimes it is known as 'Portland Trailblazer'. The petal-packed, strongly coloured, dark, carmine-red flowers are borne amid large, dark green, matt leaves.

'Blessings'

Height: 90cm (3ft)
Spread: 90cm (3ft)
This rose derives from a cross between 'Queen Elizabeth' and an unnamed seedling, and was introduced in 1968. It creates a mass of slightly fragrant, medium- to large-sized blooms. The colour is a pretty salmon-pink with a deeper colour in the centre. The medium green, glossy leaves have good resistance to diseases.

'Blue Moon'

Height: 90cm (3ft)
Spread: 75–90cm (2.5–3ft)
Derived from a cross between an unnamed seedling and 'Sterling Silver', this rose was introduced in 1964. It creates a wealth of silvery lilac, fully petalled flowers and undoubtedly is the best rose with this colour. The flowers have the bonus of a strong lemon scent. The vigorous, semi-glossy foliage is susceptible to an infection of rust.

'Bobby Charlton'

Height 90–120cm (3–4ft)
Spread: 90–100cm (3–3.5ft)
Beautiful, large, high-centred, deep pink flowers with silver reverses make this rose an ideal variety for exhibiting. The fragrance of the blooms is spicy but the blooms themselves are sometimes sparsely produced. The flowers are superbly attractive in a garden and appear amid dark green, semi-glossy leaves. In wet areas the plant is especially prone to diseases. It also has the habit of flowering slightly later than most other varieties.

It has received many awards in North America. In extremely cold winters it may need some protection.

'Buccaneer'

Height: 1.2m (4ft)
Spread: 1–1.2m (3.5–4ft)
Introduced in 1953, with 'Golden Rapture', 'Max Krause' and 'Captain Thomas' in its parentage, this Hybrid Tea bears medium-size flowers of unfading buttercup-yellow. The flowers are moderately packed with petals and borne in clusters on tall, upright stems amid medium green, matt foliage. It has the virtue of surviving rain, and is ideal for planting in a garden border.

'Chicago Peace'

Height: 90–100cm (3–3.5ft)
Spread: 90cm (3ft)
Introduced in 1962, this sport of 'Peace' has large and full blooms with orange and

'Bobby Charlton'

'Christian Dior'

'Buccaneer'

'Chicago Peace'

'Chrysler Imperial'

'Crimson Glory'

'Double Delight'

yellow shades, heavily overlaid with cyclamen-pink. It gains the first part of its name because it appeared in a Chicago garden. The large and glossy, dark green foliage is borne on tall, branching stems. It may grow taller than the listed height, depending on the vigour with which it is pruned. The more severely the stems are cut back, the taller it grows. It can then be used to create a hedge. However, it is also good in beds and for exhibiting.

'Christian Dior'
Height: 1.2m (4ft)
Spread: 1–1.2m (3.5–4ft)
Introduced in 1959 from crossings between 'Peace' and 'Happiness', and 'Independence' and 'Happiness', this tall-growing variety bears rich, velvety, scarlet blooms, which are paler on the reverse. Individual blooms are large and packed with scentless petals, and borne on upright stems bearing medium green, semi-glossy foliage which has an attractive red tinge when young. Unfortunately, it is susceptible to mildew.

'Chrysler Imperial'
Height: 90cm (3ft)
Spread: 75–90cm (2.5–3ft)
Introduced in 1952 from a cross between 'Charlotte Armstrong' and 'Mirandy', this rose develops large, richly fragrant, vividly crimson flowers with darker shading. These blooms are borne on moderately vigorous, upright stems that bear dark green,

semi-glossy foliage. It is, however, susceptible to infections of rust and mildew.

'Crimson Glory'
Height: 90cm (3ft)
Spread: 75–90cm (2.5–3ft)
'Crimson Glory' is an old variety, introduced in 1935 from a cross between a seedling of 'Catherine Kordes' and 'W. E. Chaplin'. The very fragrant, deep velvety red flowers tend to become rust-coloured with age. The blooms are freely borne amid medium green, semi-glossy leaves which are tinted red when young. This rose has subsequently been used as a parent for many other well-known roses, such as: 'Blaze Away', 'Frensham', 'Olympic Torch', and 'Madame Louis Laperrière'.

'Double Delight'
Height: 1.2m (4ft)
Spread: 90–100cm (3–3.5ft)
A beautiful American variety introduced in 1976, 'Double Delight' bears strongly scented blooms, rich cream in colour, with bold splashes of strawberry on the outer row of petals. The proportion of cream to red is not uniform; this creates a rich, variable design on each flower. Additionally, the flowers are freely produced and last for a long time. They are borne amid medium green, semi-glossy leaves. Unfortunately, this lovely rose is prone to diseases and will certainly need to be sprayed against mildew.

'Dutch Gold'
Height: 90cm (3ft)
Spread: 75–90cm (2.5–3ft)
This Hybrid Tea is a superb upright and vigorous variety. It was introduced in 1978 from a cross between 'Peer Gynt' and 'Whisky Mac'. The blooms are highly scented, large and well-formed, with a deep and unfading golden-yellow colour. They are freely borne amid medium green, glossy leaves. The plant is ideal for growing in a garden, as well as displaying in an exhibition. It is superb as a cut flower.

'Ena Harkness'
Height: 90–100cm (3–3.5ft)
Spread: 90cm (3ft)
This long-established variety was introduced in 1946 from a cross between 'Southport' and 'Crimson Glory', and for many years was one of the most popular red roses. The shapely, crimson-scarlet flowers are large and fragrant, and are borne amid medium green, semi-glossy leaves. The blooms have a superb colour, but their necks are weak, causing them to droop. However, to many rosarians this is not considered to be a problem.

'Ernest H. Morse'
Height: 90cm (3ft)
Spread: 75–90cm (2.5–3ft)
This strongly coloured rose has been popular ever since its introduction in 1965. The bright, rich turkey-red flowers are packed with petals and appear amid dark green, semi-glossy leaves. The flowers have the bonus of being scented. Plants are vigorous and the growth upright. It is used for planting in gardens, showing in exhibitions and including in floral decorations. Additionally, the flowers are borne prolifically throughout the summer season.

'Fragrant Cloud'
Height: 90cm (3ft)
Spread: 75–90cm (2.5–3ft)
'Fragrant Cloud' is also known as 'Duftwolke' and 'Nuage Parfume'. It resulted from a cross between an unnamed seedling and 'Prima Ballerina' and was introduced in 1964. It is an exceptionally fragrant variety, bearing large, well-formed, coral-scarlet flowers with smoky overtones. The very strong, upright stems are clothed with large, glossy, dark green leaves. Unfortunately, it may need spraying against black spot disease.

Although the fame of this rose has declined in recent years, it is still worthy of inclusion in a rose garden, especially one that is fragrant.

'Grandpa Dickson'
Height: 90cm (3ft)
Spread: 75–90cm (2.5–3ft)
Introduced in 1966, with 'Perfecta', 'Governador Braga da Cruz' and 'Piccadilly' in its parentage, this rose is also called 'Irish Gold'. It has a superb pale lemon-yellow colour, fading to creamy yellow with age, and flushed pink at the

'Dutch Gold'

'Ernest H. Morse'

'Fragrant Cloud'

edges of the petals. The flowers are very shapely and borne on tall, upright stems bearing glossy, dark green foliage. It needs to be planted in rich soil and fed regularly if a spare appearance is to be avoided. It is tolerant of both drought and wet weather. This is a rose that can be planted to create wonderful colour, shape and texture combinations.

'Helen Traubel'
Height: 1.2m (4ft)
Spread: 90–100cm (3–3.5ft)
Introduced in 1951 from a cross between 'Charlotte Armstrong' and 'Glowing Sunset', this Hybrid Tea has fragrant, coppery pink flowers suffused with an apricot colour, which look especially beautiful in autumn. The flowers are carried on tall and vigorous stems which are clothed with attractive dark green, matt foliage.

During exceptionally warm weather, the flowers open very rapidly.

'John Waterer'
Height: 75cm (2.5ft)
Spread: 60–75cm (2–2.5ft)
Introduced in 1970, this vigorous and branching rose bears superbly coloured, midsummer-flowering red roses. Although the flowers have only a slight fragrance, they are beautiful in shape and form. Their red colour makes them a strong feature in a rose garden.

'Ena Harkness'

'Helen Traubel'

'Grandpa Dickson'

'John Waterer'

'Josephine Bruce'

Height: 75cm (2.5ft)
Spread: 75cm (2.5ft)

This is an outstandingly attractive introduction from 1952, and a result of a cross between 'Crimson Glory' and 'Madge Whipp'. With a spreading stance, it bears highly fragrant, shapely, deep crimson flowers, sometimes flushed dark scarlet. The dark green, semi-glossy foliage is borne on slightly sprawling shoots. For that reason, these rose plants are best pruned to inward-pointed buds to encourage a less lax and spreading stance.

Unfortunately, the blooms are easily damaged by rain, and the foliage is likely to become infected with mildew. It may be necessary to spray against mildew. Do not plant it in excessively wet areas.

'Just Joey'

Height: 75–90cm (2.5–3ft)
Spread: 75–90cm (2.5–3ft)

A uniquely coloured rose, 'Just Joey' is a cross between 'Fragrant Cloud' and 'Dr. Verhage', and was introduced in the early 1970s. The fragrant, coppery orange flowers, veined in red, have ruffled petals. Flowers are borne over a long period and are ideal as cut flowers. The flowers are weather-resistant and continue into autumn. It is ideal for planting in rose beds, and has received many awards. It is not, however, suitable for showing.

'Josephine Bruce'

'Just Joey'

'King's Ransom'

'Korp'

'Kronenbourg'

'Lady Sylvia'

'Lolita'

'King's Ransom'
Height: 90cm (3ft)
Spread: 75cm (2.5ft)
This Hybrid Tea is a superb yellow rose. It was introduced in 1961 from a cross between 'Golden Masterpiece' and 'Lydia'. The fragrant, rich yellow flowers are beautifully shaped, do not fade, and are ideal for cutting. Unfortunately, the dark green, glossy growth tends to be straggly. Avoid planting it in chalky soils or those with a sandy nature. It has won many awards, both in Britain and North America.

'Korp'
Height: 75–90cm (2.5–3ft)
Spread: 60–75cm (2–2.5ft)
Also known as 'Prominent' and introduced in 1970 from a cross between 'Colour Wonder' and 'Zorina', this Hybrid Tea has proved to be a distinctive rose. The double, vermilion flowers are borne in clusters of four or five, amid matt green leaves. Growth is normally upright and bushy. It is ideal in flower arrangements, as well as for planting in rose beds. Additionally, it grows well in pots in the greenhouse.

'Kronenbourg'
Height: 1.2m (4ft)
Spread: 90–100cm (3–3.5ft)
Also known as 'Flaming Peace', this 1965 introduction is a sport of 'Peace', to which it sometimes reverts. The large and full, slightly fragrant flowers are scarlet on the inside and yellow on the reverse, creating a very attractive effect. The growth is vigorous, with dark green, glossy leaves. Unfortunately, with age the blooms tend to fade and discolour, making dead-heading a regular and essential job. Nevertheless, it is well worth growing for its bicoloured blooms.

'Lady Sylvia'
Height: 90–120cm (3–4ft)
Spread: 75–90cm (2.5–3ft)
Introduced in 1927 as a sport from 'Madame Butterfly', this old variety still generates interest to rose growers. It is ideal for planting in rose beds, as well as for cut flowers. The shapely, highly fragrant flowers are light rose-pink, shading to pale apricot-yellow at their bases. They are borne on strong, long, upright stems, amid matt green foliage. It has the bonus of bearing flowers into autumn.

'Lolita'
Height: 75–90cm (2.5–3ft)
Spread: 75–90cm (2.5–3ft)
This is a superb rose, with rich, highly fragrant, golden apricot flowers borne amid upright, thorn-clad stems that display coppery leaves. Additionally, it is able to withstand mildew, black spot disease and cold weather. Because of its unique colouring of blooms and leaves, and because of its scent, flower arrangers find it very useful in arrangements.

'Message'
Height: 75cm (2.5ft)
Spread: 75cm (2.5ft)
Also known as 'White Knight' and introduced in 1956 from a cross between 'Virgo' and 'Peace', this lovely rose bears large, shapely, pure white flowers with high centres.

The blooms are borne on long, erect stems. The growth is vigorous, with light green, matt leaves. Unfortunately, it is susceptible to mildew and rust, and may need regular spraying to keep it healthy. Additionally, the flowers are frequently damaged by heavy showers of rain.

It has been acclaimed in both Europe and North America and has received several awards.

'Mister Lincoln'
Height: 1.2m (4ft)
Spread: 75–90cm (2.5–3ft)
Introduced in 1964 from a cross between 'Chrysler Imperial' and 'Charles Mallerin', 'Mister Lincoln' is widely acclaimed in North America. The large, full, velvet-like, slightly fragrant, dark crimson flowers are suffused with scarlet. The growth is vigorous, with dark green, matt leaves. It needs to be planted in a large bed. It is susceptible to mildew.

In North America it has not proved to be as hardy as originally thought, but nevertheless it does appear to be a survivor. It is unsuitable for planting in small rose beds.

'Mojave'
Height: 90cm (3ft)
Spread: 75–90cm (2.5–3ft)
'Mojave' is derived from a cross between 'Charlotte Armstrong' and 'Signora', and was introduced in 1954. It forms a very hardy plant, with exceptionally fragrant, rich burnt-orange and reddish flame flowers with darker veining. The glossy, bronze-green leaves are borne on leggy and lax plants. It is a healthy plant, excelling in autumn. It has been the recipient of many awards.

'Mrs Sam McGredy'
Height: 90cm (3ft)
Spread: 75–90cm (2.5–3ft)
This rose is an old variety, but nevertheless not without its admirers. It was introduced in 1929 as a result of a cross between 'Donald Macdonald' and 'Golden Emblem', and a seedling and 'The Queen Alexandra Rose'. The bright coppery scarlet and salmon-red flowers are beautifully formed and borne on long stems. The leaves are also attractive, having a copper-beech shade. Like many old varieties it needs regular feeding and care, as well as protection against black spo disease. It is ideal for planting in rose beds.

'Mullard Jubilee'
Height: 90cm (3ft)
Spread: 75cm (2.5ft)
Also known as 'Electron', this is a 1970 introduction. The flowers are freely produced, large, deeply

'Message'

'Mister Lincoln'

'Mojave'

'Mrs Sam McGredy'

'Mullard Jubilee'

'Papa Meilland'

'Paradise'

fragrant and an attractive shade of rose-pink. They are carried in clusters. It is vigorous, with dark green, semi-glossy foliage and a compact nature. Although flowers are resistant to rain damage, spraying against rust may be necessary.

'Papa Meilland'
Height: 90cm (3ft)
Spread: 75cm (2.5ft)
Introduced in 1963 from a cross between 'Chrysler Imperial' and 'Charles Mallerin', this rose creates an unfortunate paradox for many rose enthusiasts. The flowers are full, superbly fragrant and a dark velvety crimson, but the plant in general is not reliable and very prone to mildew. The growth is generally vigorous and upright, with dark green glossy leaves. However, it confirms the fact that if the colour appeals, it is very difficult to diminish a rose's popularity.

'Paradise'
Height: 90–100cm
(3–3.5ft)
Spread: 90cm (3ft)
This superb rose was introduced in 1978. The buds open to silvery lavender, with the edges of petals becoming a ruby red colour which gradually spreads over the entire flower. The blooms are slightly scented and borne amid glossy, deep green leaves. It is resistant to diseases and also appears to be tolerant of cold winters.

'Pascali'
*Height: 90–100cm
(3– 3.5ft)*
Spread: 75–90cm (2.5–3ft)
Introduced in 1963 from a
cross between 'Queen
Elizabeth' and 'White
Butterfly', 'Pascali' has been
popular for many years. The
scentless white flowers, first
shaded peach, are borne on
tall, upright stems clothed
with semi-glossy, dark green
leaves. The flowers are
relatively resistant to rain
and mildew. Plant the foam
flower (*Tiarella cordifolia*)
around the stems to create
more colour.

'Peace'
*Height: 100–120cm
(3.5– 4ft)*
*Spread: 90–100cm
(3– 3.5ft)*
Perhaps one of the best-
known roses, 'Peace' was
introduced in 1942 and was
bought in millions after the
Second World War. Also
known as 'Gloria Dei', it has
several well-known roses in
its parentage, including
'Joanna Hill', 'Charles P.
Kilham', 'Margaret McGredy'
and *Rosa foetida bicolor*. The
large, globular and rather
heavy blooms are light
yellow – sometimes deeper
in later flushes in autumn –
and occasionally tinged
pink. The flowers are
especially attractive when
fully open. They are borne
amid vigorous and
branching, leathery, dark
green and glossy foliage.
Because of its vigorous
stance, it should only be
lightly pruned.

'Pascali'

'Peace'

'Peer Gynt'

'Prima Ballerina'

'Piccadilly'

'Pink Peace'

'Red Devil'

'Peer Gynt'

Height: 90cm (3ft)
Spread: 75cm (2.5ft)
This brightly coloured rose was introduced in 1968 from a cross between 'Colour Wonder' and 'Golden Giant'. The slightly fragrant, globular, canary-yellow flowers are tinged orange-pink on the edges of the outer petals. It creates a bushy plant, with light green, matt leaves. It is ideal for planting in rose beds, but unfortunately is not particularly resistant to mildew.

'Piccadilly'

Height: 75cm (2.5ft)
Spread: 60–75cm (2–2.5ft)
Introduced in 1959 from a cross between 'McGredy's Yellow' and 'Karl Herbst', it is one of the best bicoloured varieties. The slightly fragrant blooms are scarlet and gold, and with age these colours fade and merge. The blooms are borne amid bronze-tinted, glossy foliage. The plant's compact and free-flowering characteristics make it ideal for planting in rose beds, but unfortunately it is not resistant to diseases. It is yet another rose that has received many awards.

'Pink Peace'

Height: 90–100cm (3–3.5ft)
Spread: 90cm (3ft)
As its name suggests, this rose owes part of its parentage to 'Peace', as well as to 'Monique' and 'Mrs John Laing'. It was introduced in 1959. The large, slightly cupped, fragrant, deep pink flowers are full and borne on bushy, upright stems. These are surrounded by bronze-tinted, semi-glossy, disease-resistant leaves.

'Prima Ballerina'

Height: 90–100cm (3–3.5ft)
Spread: 75–90cm (2.5–3ft)
Also known as 'Premiere Ballerine', this Hybrid Tea was introduced in 1958 from a cross between an unknown seedling and 'Peace'. The shapely, richly fragrant, bright pink flowers become rose-pink and are borne on tall, vigorous stems. The foliage is light green and semi-glossy. Unfortunately, it is becoming more susceptible to damage from rain, as well as to mildew. Regular spraying may be necessary.

'Red Devil'

Height: 100cm (3.5ft)
Spread: 75–90cm (2.5–3ft)
Also known as 'Coeur d'Amour', this rose was introduced in 1967 from a cross between 'Silver Lining' and 'Prima Ballerina'. It is a superb exhibition rose. The strongly fragrant, large, glowing scarlet flowers have a distinctly light reverse. Each bloom is packed with petals and borne on stiff, upright stems amid rich green, glossy leaves. It is an ideal rose bush for planting in rose beds, where the flowers are freely borne, but it tends to be damaged by rain.

'Red Lion'

Height: 75–90cm (2.5–3ft)
Spread: 75–90cm (2.5–3ft)
'Red Lion' is a bright, cherry-red rose with highly reflexed flowers. It is ideal in both hot and cool areas, with the flowers retaining their attractive nature in varying climates. The upright and vigorous foliage has a leathery texture. This rose will add strong and stunning colour to a garden flower bed.

'Rose Gaujard'

Height: 100cm (3.5ft)
Spread: 75–90cm (2.5–3ft)
Introduced in 1958 from a cross between 'Peace' and a seedling of 'Opera', this Hybrid Tea develops masses of slightly fragrant, cherry-red blooms with silvery white reverses. The growth is vigorous and tall-branching, with dark green, glossy leaves frequently tinted bronze.

Along with being free-flowering, it is also resistant to diseases. It is ideal for planting in rose beds and is attractive in autumn.

'Royal Highness'

Height: 90–100cm (3–3.5ft)
Spread: 90cm (3ft)
Introduced in 1962 from a cross between 'Virgo' and 'Peace', this rose bears high-centred, full-petalled, fragrant, soft pink flowers. The growth is vigorous and branching, with dark green, glossy leaves.

Unfortunately, it is soon spoilt by rain, especially prolonged rainy spells, and

therefore best grown in relatively dry areas.

In North America it has been given several awards, and is hardy in even the coldest of places. It is sometimes known as 'Konigliche Hoheit'.

'Shot Silk'

Height: 75cm (2.5ft)
Spread: 60–75cm (2–2.5ft)
'Shot Silk' is an old variety, but still acclaimed by many rosarians. The large, petal-packed, high-centred, salmon-pink flowers shaded gold are eye-catching and very fragrant. It certainly deserves its name for its shimmering flowers. Blooms appear amid medium green, glossy leaves. Regrettably, it is a variety that has lost some of its vigour through the years. It can also be grown in its climbing form.

'Silver Jubilee'

Height: 75cm (2.5ft)
Spread: 60–75cm (2–2.5ft)
This universally acclaimed rose was introduced in 1978 and since then has received many awards. Although a relatively recent variety, it has gained an admiring following among rosarians. The remarkable colour and healthy nature of this rose bush are appealing characteristics.

The beautiful flowers are scented, coppery salmon-pink and shaded with peach and cream. Plants are free-flowering, with medium green, glossy, disease-resistant leaves. It is ideal for

'Red Lion'

'Rose Gaujard'

'Silver Jubilee'

'Royal Highness'

'Silver Lining'

'Shot Silk'

'Summer Sunshine'

planting in rose beds, but because of its short flower stems it is not popular with flower arrangers.

'Silver Lining'
Height: 75–90cm (2.5–3ft)
Spread: 75cm (2.5ft)
Introduced in 1958 from a cross between 'Karl Herbst' and a seedling of 'Eden Rose', this Hybrid Tea is ideal for planting in rose beds, as well as for exhibiting. It is widely used in flower arrangements. The exceedingly fragrant, shapely flowers have graceful, reflexing petals, silvery pink on the inside, with a silver reverse. The foliage is rather small, dark green and glossy. Unfortunately, when in a garden, the individual flowers do not create an impact of colour, but individually and indoors they are eye-catching.

'Summer Sunshine'
Height: 75–90cm (2.5–3ft)
Spread: 75cm (2.5ft)
Also known as 'Soleil d'Été, this 1962 introduction from a cross between 'Buccaneer' and 'Lemon Chiffon' has medium-sized, petal-packed, slightly fragrant, deep yellow flowers with large petals. The blooms are carried on long stems amid dark green, glossy leaves. Unfortunately, although the flowers are attractive and richly coloured, plants are often short-lived.

'Super Star'
Height: 90–100cm (3–3.5ft)
Spread: 90cm (3ft)
Introduced in 1960 from a cross between 'Peace' and an unnamed seedling, and 'Alpine Glow' and another seedling, this is a well known and widely grown rose. It has won many awards, with world-wide acclaim for the light vermilion flowers that have a fluorescent glow. Additionally, flowers are fragrant and shapely, and carried on tall, upright stems amid medium green, semi-glossy leaves. The long stems make it ideal for cutting, as well as for planting in rose beds. Unfortunately, it is susceptible to mildew. It is sometimes known as 'Tropicana'.

'Sutter's Gold'
Height: 75–90cm (2.5–3ft)
Spread: 75cm (2.5ft)
Introduced in 1950 from a cross between 'Charlotte Armstrong' and 'Signora', this widely acclaimed rose has very fragrant, petal-packed, shapely flowers. The blooms are a deep rich gold in colour flushed with peach. They are carried on tall, erect stems, making them ideal for cutting. The growth is sometimes gaunt, lax and spindly, with dark green, glossy leaves.

'Tenerife'
Height: 90cm (3ft)
Spread: 75cm (2.5ft)
With parents 'Fragrant Cloud' and 'Piccadilly', this

'Super Star'

'Tenerife'

'Sutter's Gold'

'Troika'

96

Wendy Cussons'

Whisky Mac'

award-winning rose is highly attractive. The petal-packed, deep coral-salmon petals have peach reverses and are very fragrant. Blooms are borne amid medium green, glossy leaves. Unfortunately, it is not noted for its resistance to rain, and is susceptible to diseases. Nevertheless, the flowers are very attractive, although the colour tends to be variable.

'Troika'
Height: 90cm (3ft)
Spread: 75cm (2.5ft)
Also known as 'Royal Dane' and introduced in 1972 from unknown parentage, this elegant rose is ideal for planting in rose beds, as well as for exhibiting and cutting for room decoration. Its fragrant, large, petal-packed, orange-bronze flowers are shaded red and borne amid medium green, glossy leaves. The growth is vigorous and upright. Flowers do not fade and are resistant to damage from rain. This rose is also resistant to diseases.

'Wendy Cussons'
Height: 90–100cm (3–3.5ft)
Spread: 90cm (3ft)
This world-famous rose was introduced in 1959 from a cross between 'Independence' and 'Eden Rose'. The large, petal-packed flowers are perfectly formed, richly scented with a Damask-like fragrance, and superbly coloured a deep reddish pink. The growth is vigorous and branching. Dark green, glossy leaves have a slight reddish tinge. Additionally, it is resistant to weather damage.

'Whisky Mac'
Height: 75cm (2.5ft)
Spread: 75cm (2.5ft)
Introduced in 1968, 'Whisky Mac' is now one of the most popular Hybrid Teas. The very fragrant, petal-packed, deep gold flowers are overlaid with orange and bronze. They appear amid dark green, glossy leaves which are tinted bronze when young. However, it needs good soil, and is susceptible to mildew.

Other recommended Hybrid Teas:

'Adolf Horstmann'	'Diorama'	'Mon Cheri'
'Alpine Sunset'	'First Prize'	'Oregold'
'Anastasia'	'Flaming Beauty'	'Pink Favourite'
'Bewitched'	'Friendship'	'Precious Platinum'
'Big Purple'	'Gambler's Special'	'Royal William'
'Broadway'	'Granada'	'Sheer Bliss'
'Canadian White Star'	'Honor'	'Sunblest'
'Captain Harry Stebbings'	'John F. Kennedy'	'Swarthmore'
'Chivalry'	'Medallion'	'Tiffany'
'Dolce Vita'	'Mischief'	'Virgo'

Floribunda Roses

These roses are now known as Cluster-flowered Bush Roses. They are hardy, deciduous shrubs, derived from crosses between the early Hybrid Teas and Dwarf Polyanthas. They are therefore later in origin than Hybrid Teas. Floribundas bear their flowers in clusters, and although the individual flowers are generally smaller than those on Hybrid Teas, they are often highly colourful and borne in flushes throughout summer and into autumn.

Recently introduced Floribundas have larger flowers and increasing amounts of scent. In general, the plants are strong, reliable and easy to grow. They soon bring colour to gardens.

'Amber Queen'

'Apricot Nectar'

'Arcadian'

'Arthur Bell'

'Amber Queen'
Height: 60cm (2ft)
Spread: 45–60cm (1.5–2ft)
Introduced in 1984 from a cross between 'Southampton' and 'Typhoon', and also known as 'Harooney', this star of the rose world has received many awards, including Rose of the Year. The petal-packed, amber-yellow flowers are large and attractively cup-shaped when fully open. They have the bonus of being scented. Each truss bears many individual flowers, amid dark green, glossy leaves on plants that are bushy and moderately vigorous.

'Apricot Nectar'
Height: 1–1.2m (3.5–4ft)
Spread: 90cm–1m (3–3.5ft)
This vigorous 1965 introduction resulted from a cross between 'Spartan' and an unnamed seedling. The pale apricot flowers, shading to gold at their bases, are packed with petals and open to about 10cm (4in) wide. These are borne on tall,

upright shoots that have medium green, glossy leaves. Unfortunately, it is likely to become infected with mildew, so regular spraying is necessary. It is, however, a magnificent Floribunda.

'Arcadian'
Height: 90–100cm (3–3.5ft)
Spread: 90cm (3ft)
Also known as 'Macnewye' and 'New Year', this rose was introduced in 1982 from a cross between 'Mary Sumner' and an unnamed seedling. The slightly scented, large, strongly blush-orange flowers are borne amid dark, bronze-green, glossy leaves. Plants are usually healthy.

'Arthur Bell'
Height: 90–100cm (3–3.5ft)
Spread: 90cm (3ft)
Introduced in 1965, from a cross between 'Cläre Grammerstorf' and 'Piccadilly', this superbly scented rose bears large, semi-double, golden yellow

'Bonfire Night'

'Bright Smile'

flowers that become cup-shaped when fully open. With age, the flowers fade to cream. The pronounced fragrance is, perhaps, the main attraction of this Floribunda. The flowers are borne amid medium green, glossy leaves that are resistant to mildew and black spot disease. It also has the virtue of a long flowering period, starting early and continuing well into autumn.

'Bonfire Night'
Height: 75cm (2.5ft)
Spread: 75cm (2.5ft)
Introduced in 1970 from a cross between 'Tiki' and 'Variety Club', this Floribunda forms a superbly bushy plant with attractive dark green leaves. The leaves create a foil for the orange-scarlet flowers, which are further highlighted by lighter reverses. The flowers are borne in large trusses and create a wonderful display.

'Bright Smile'
Height: 60cm (2ft)
Spread: 45–50cm
  (18–20in)
Introduced in the early part of the 1980s from a cross between 'Eurorose' and an unnamed seedling, this rose is acknowledged as a superb yellow-flowered Floribunda, albeit with rather lax flowers. The blooms are produced in masses. It starts flowering early, amid medium green, glossy leaves that are resistant to diseases.

'Brown Velvet'

Height: 90–100cm (3–3.5ft)
Spread: 90cm (3ft)
This 1979 New Zealand Gold Medal Winner is stunningly attractive, with small, orange-red flowers borne in clusters of three or five on upright stems. It was raised from a cross between 'Mary Sumner' and 'Kapai'. In cool weather the flowers assume a purplish cast that, in some circumstances, appears as a brownish hue. The plants are further highlighted by dark green leaves that are resistant to disease.

'Centurion'

Height: 90–120cm
  (3–3.5ft)
Spread: 75–90cm (2.5–3ft)
Introduced in 1975 from a cross between 'Evelyn Fison' and an unnamed seedling, this rose creates a wealth of slightly scented, large, gloriously bright, red flowers amid medium green leaves. The colour is so strong that it can dominate a rose bed, and in poor light may appear very dark.

'Circus'

Height: 90cm (3ft)
Spread: 75–90cm (2.5–3ft)
A superb Floribunda Rose, 'Circus' was introduced in 1955 from a cross between 'Fandango' and 'Pinnocchio'. It has proved to be ideal for gardens, winning many awards. The petal-packed flowers, pink with salmon suffusions, are borne in fairly large clusters. These colour overtones spread as the flowers age. Flowers

'Brown Velvet'

'Centurion'

'Circus'

'City of Leeds'

'Congratulations'

'Elizabeth of Glamis'

'Europeana'

have the bonus of a sweet and spicy redolence. It has a branching habit, with dark green, glossy leaves. It may need protection against black spot disease, but has the advantage of flowering up until early winter.

'City of Leeds'
Height: 75cm (2.5ft)
Spread: 60cm (2ft)
This widely grown and popular variety was introduced in 1966 from a cross between 'Evelyn Fison' and a further liaison between 'Spartan' and 'Red Favourite' and has few rivals when a massed display of rich salmon-pink is desired. Additionally, the fragrant flowers are borne in large sprays amid dark green, semi-glossy, small leaves.

'Congratulations'
Height: 1m (3.5ft)
Spread: 90cm (3ft)
Also known as 'Korlift' and sometimes classified as a Hybrid Tea type, this rose displays elegant and delicately coloured, slightly fragrant flowers borne in small clusters. The blooms are rose-pink and packed with petals, and appear amid medium green, semi-glossy leaves on vigorous and upright plants. With age the flowers lose their colour and become pale, but they do continue into autumn.

The plant was raised from a cross between 'Carina' and an unnamed seedling. It is generally resistant to most diseases.

'Elizabeth of Glamis'
Height: 50–60cm
(20–24in)
Spread: 45–50cm
(18–20in)
Also known as 'Irish Beauty' and introduced in 1964 from a cross between 'Spartan' and 'Highlight', this Floribunda has long been appreciated for its wonderful cinnamon-scented, salmon-pink flowers that are borne in small clusters. The foliage is dark green and semi-glossy. It needs to be planted in good soil; avoid cold clay soil that tends to inhibit early growth. Only plant it in good soil and spray against diseases.

'Europeana'
Height: 50–60cm
(20–24in)
Spread: 45–50cm
(18–20in)
An introduction from 1963, 'Europeana' was raised from a cross between 'Ruth Leuwevak' and 'Rosemary Rose'. It is superb when planted *en masse*, but take care not to position the plants more than 50cm (20in) apart so that the spreading shoots can support each other. The petal-packed, deep crimson, fully double flowers are borne in large trusses. Additionally, the flowers are fragrant and the foliage a deep reddish purple when young, slowly changing to bronze-green. Because the plant is packed with foliage, spray regularly as a measure against mildew.

'Evelyn Fison'
Height: 75cm (2.5ft)
Spread: 50–60cm
(20– 24in)
Also known as 'Irish Wonder', this 1962 introduction is well established as a reliable, vivid scarlet Floribunda, well-worth growing for its large, scented flower trusses. It originated from a cross between 'Moulin Rouge' and 'Korona'. The dark green, disease-resistant foliage, borne on branching shoots, is also attractive. Additionally, the flowers are not damaged by cold and wet weather.

'Eye Paint'
Height: 120cm (4ft)
Spread: 90–120cm (3–4ft)
This very vigorous rose was introduced in 1976, from a cross between 'Picasso' and an unnamed seedling. The small, single, bright scarlet flowers have white eyes and golden stamens, and are borne amid medium green, semi-glossy leaves. The flowers are devoid of scent. Its height and vigour make it superb for a hedge.

'Fragrant Delight'
Height: 75cm (2.5ft)
Spread: 60cm (2ft)
As its name suggests, this rose is richly scented, with the bonus of beautiful coppery salmon flowers that shade to yellow at their bases. The size and shape of the flowers has encouraged several rose nurseries to include it with Hybrid Teas. It was introduced in the

1970s, from a cross between 'Chanelle' and 'Whisky Mac' The blooms are further highlighted by the attractive bronze-green young leaves that slowly turn mid-green.

'Frensham'
Height: 1.2m (4ft)
Spread: 1–1.2m (3.5–4ft)
Introduced in 1946 from a cross between an unnamed seedling and 'Crimson Glory', this Floribunda has a slightly Hybrid Tea appearance to its deep scarlet-crimson, semi-double flowers that appear well spaced in their trusses. The flowers are borne on branching stems amid glossy green leaves which need to be sprayed regularly as a preventative measure against mildew.

'Golden Slippers'
Height: 45cm (1.5ft)
Spread: 45cm (1.5ft)
Introduced in the United States of America in 1961, it resulted from a cross between 'Goldilocks' and an unnamed seedling. Its small stature has made it ideal for planting along the edges of patios. The Hybrid Tea-shaped flowers have orange-flame interiors, with pale gold reverses. Unfortunately, the fragrant flowers fade quickly. The growth is bushy, with glossy green leaves that are, regrettably, susceptible to black spot. Additionally, it needs fertile soil and cool weather – in hot, dry summers it is unreliable.

'Evelyn Fison'

'Eye Paint'

'Fragrant Delight'

'Frensham'

'Golden Slippers'

'Iceberg'

'Intrigue'

'Iceberg'

Height: 1.2m (4ft)
Spread: 1–1.2m (3.5–4ft)

Also known as 'Schneewittchen' and introduced in 1958 from a cross between 'Robin Hood' and 'Virgo', this is often thought to be an ideal white Floribunda Rose. The buds are tinted pink, but open to reveal fragrant, pure white blooms borne in medium to large trusses. During late summer, the flowers may become tinged pink. It flowers throughout summer and often until the onset of severe winter weather. The foliage is medium green and glossy. If the plant is only lightly pruned, it will form a small shrub, ideal for planting in a border. It needs to be sprayed against mildew and black spot.

'Intrigue'

Height: 90cm (3ft)
Spread: 75–90cm (2.5–3ft)

This fascinating and unusual dark-faced rose was introduced in North America in 1983 and each year it increases in popularity. Its parents are 'White Masterpiece' and 'Heirloom'. The deep, plum-purple, slightly ruffled flowers are borne in small clusters on long stems. This rose is further admired for its bouquet. The foliage is resistant to diseases.

An earlier 'Intrigue' is pictured here. It was raised in 1973 from a cross between 'Grüss an Bayern' and a seedling and produces dark red blooms.

'Irish Mist'

Height: 90cm (3ft)
Spread: 75–90cm (2.5–3ft)
A beautifully named
introduction from 1967 and
the result of a cross between
'Orangeade' and 'Mischief'
This rose is a Grandiflora
type. The relatively recent
Grandiflora grouping
includes roses derived from
crossings between modern
Hybrid Teas and modern
Floribundas. The superbly
formed flowers have a
Hybrid Tea structure and
reveal a beautiful orange-
salmon tone, and are
characterized by having
serrated edges to the petals.
Plants are moderately
vigorous, with a branching
habit and bearing dark
green, semi-glossy leaves.

'Isis'

Height: 90–100cm (3–3.5ft)
Spread: 75–90cm (2.5–3ft)
This was introduced in 1973
from a cross between 'Vera
Dalton' and 'Shepherdess'.
The beautiful, well-shaped,
delightfully fragrant, double
ivory-white flowers open to
about 10cm (4in) wide.
These pale blooms are
borne on bushy yet compact
plants, with medium green,
glossy leaves.

'Korresia'

Height: 75cm (2.5ft)
Spread: 60–75cm (2–2.5ft)
Also known as 'Friesia' and
'Sunsprite' and introduced
in 1973, this is one of the
best yellow-flowered
Floribundas. The large,
petal-packed and fragrant
flowers have the virtue of

'Irish Mist'

'Isis'

'Lilli Marlene'

'Korresia'

'Margaret Merrill'

'Masquerade'

'Matangi'

not fading. The medium green, glossy foliage is relatively disease resistant and borne on bushy plants. Flower arrangers enjoy this rose, as the buds open slowly and last a long time.

'Lilli Marlene'
Height: 75cm (2.5ft)
Spread: 60–75cm (2–2.5ft)
This 1959 introduction from a cross between 'Our Princess' and 'Rudolph Timm' is ideal when planted in a rose bed. It creates a mass of semi-double, slightly fragrant, rounded, deep scarlet flowers with crimson shading. Blooms are borne well above the medium green, semi-glossy leaves. It is reliable and free-flowering, with branching stems bearing medium green, glossy leaves.

'Margaret Merrill'
Height: 75–90cm (2.5–3ft)
Spread: 75cm (2.5 ft)
This 1977 introduction resulted from a cross between 'Rudolph Timm' and a further liaison between 'Dedication' and 'Pascali'. It is also known as 'Harkuly'. Dainty, high-centred buds open to pearly white and are overlaid with a satiny pink sheen. These exceptional, sweetly fragrant flowers are borne in small trusses amid dark green, glossy leaves. Its failing is a susceptibility to diseases and rain, which soon spoils the flowers. However, it has been acclaimed by rosarians and given several awards.

'Masquerade'
Height: 90–100cm (3–3.5ft)
Spread: 90cm (3ft)
Few roses are as well-known as this 1950 introduction, one of the first multi-coloured varieties. It originated from a cross between 'Goldilock' and 'Holiday'. The rather lax, scented, semi-double flowers are yellow and display a pink flush, and with maturity become dull red. These colourful blooms are borne on branching shoots amid dark green and glossy leaves. The regular removal of dead flowers is essential to encourage further blooms. For many years it has proved itself to be worthy of inclusion in any garden.

'Matangi'
Height: 90cm (3ft)
Spread: 75cm (2.5ft)
This beautiful rose has received many awards for its remarkable colouring. Its slightly scented, vermilion flowers with silver reverses have white eyes. It originated from a cross between an unnamed seedling and 'Picasso'. Indeed, it strongly resembles 'Picasso'. The flowers are borne in small trusses that create a superb rose for planting in a rose bed. The foliage is dark green and glossy. Unfortunately for flower arrangers, the blooms do not last long in water, although in general the plant is resistant to damage from rain.

'Memento'
Height: 75cm (2.5ft)
Spread: 60–75cm (2–2.5ft)
Also known as 'Dicbar', and raised from 'Bangor' and 'Korbell', this Floribunda Rose produces masses of slightly fragrant, flat-faced, salmon-vermilion, medium-sized flowers on a compact bush. The trusses continue to appear throughout summer, amid medium green, glossy leaves, and the blooms are said to have a high resistance to rain. It is best planted in a rose bed.

'Moon Maiden'
Height: 75cm (2.5ft)
Spread: 60–75cm (2–2.5ft)
Raised from a cross between 'Fred Streeter' and 'All Gold', this Floribunda was introduced in 1970. The double, large, gloriously cream-yellow flowers are borne amid dark, glossy green leaves. Flowers often have attractive deeper shadings. The trusses are large, with flowers borne over a long period. Plants are bushy, tall and branching with semi-glossy leaves. Fragrance is another of its virtues.

'Mountbatten'
Height: 1.2m (4ft)
Spread: 1–1.2m (3.5–4ft)
This superb variety, also known as 'Harmantelle', was introduced in 1982 and is now widely acclaimed by rosarians. Its parentage is complex, and includes 'Peer Gynt', 'Anne Cocker', 'Arthur Bell' and 'Southampton'. It is strong and vigorous, with a shrub-like stance, bearing fragrant, petal-packed, mimosa-yellow flowers. The foliage is medium green and glossy and borne on vigorous shoots that make it ideal for growing as a hedge or for planting in a shrub border. Ensure that it has space.

'Old Master'
Height: 1–1.2m (3.5–4ft)
Spread: 90cm (3ft)
Introduced in 1974, this rose has 'Maxi', 'Evelyn Fison', 'Orange Sweetheart', 'Frühlingsmorgen', 'Tantau's Triumph', 'Coryana', 'Hamburger Phoenix' and 'Danse du Feu' in its parentage. The gloriously coloured flowers are held in large clusters, with each flower opening flat and revealing deep carmine petals with a whitish silvery eye and beautiful silvery white reverses. These are borne amid dark green, glossy leaves. It is a very healthy rose.

'Orangeade'
Height: 75cm (2.5ft)
Spread: 75cm (2.5ft)
Introduced in 1959 from a cross between 'Orange Sweetheart' and 'Independence', 'Orangeade' has been a popular rose for many years. It displays masses of brilliant orange-vermilion, semi-double flowers in large and lax trusses. To ensure continuity of roses, it is essential to remove dead flowers. The foliage is dark green and semi-glossy and

'Memento'

'Moon Maiden'

'Mountbatten'

'Old Master'

'Orangeade'

'Picasso'

'Paddy McGredy'

borne on vigorous, branching shoots. Unfortunately, it is rather susceptible to rust, mildew and black spot.

'Paddy McGredy'

Height: 60cm (2ft)
Spread: 45–50cm
(18–20in)

The flowers on this 1962 introduction are large, but the plant's stance is small. It originated from a cross between 'Spartan' and 'Tzigane'. The deep carmine-pink flowers, with paler reverses, are petal-packed and well-shaped, with the first flush often completely covering the dark green, semi-glossy leaves. Often, subsequent flushes are slow to develop. Unfortunately, the flowers tend to fade in hot and direct sunlight, and plants in general are not resistant to diseases.

'Picasso'

Height: 75cm (2.5ft)
Spread: 60cm (2ft)

Introduced in 1971, with 'Marlene', 'Evelyn Fison', 'Orange Sensation' and 'Frühlingsmorgen' in its parentage, 'Picasso' is said to be the first of the 'hand-painted' roses. It has deep pink petals, blotched red, on a white background, with the addition of silver reverses. The blooms have no fragrance and are borne on short, bushy plants with slender stems carrying medium green, matt foliage. The flowers are produced over a long season.

'Pink Parfait'
Height: 90cm (3ft)
Spread: 75cm (2.5ft)
A highly acclaimed rose, introduced in 1962 and popular ever since. It is a cross between 'First Love' and 'Pinocchio'. When in bud, the pink buds resemble those of Hybrid Teas, opening to reveal cream at their bases. The sweetly scented flowers are ideal for cutting and are borne on robust growth, carrying medium green, semi-glossy leaves. It flowers prolifically and is ideal for planting in a rose bed or border. It is also resistant to damage from rain.

'Queen Elizabeth'
Height: 1.5–1.8m (5–6ft) or more
Spread: 1–1.2m (3.5–4ft)
Introduced in 1955 from a cross between 'Charlotte Armstrong' and 'Floradora', this North American rose has been adored by rosarians ever since. It is an extremely vigorous variety, ideal for creating a pretty hedge or for planting in a shrub border.

The slightly fragrant, light pink flowers are packed with petals, forming large blooms. An additional quality is the dark green foliage that is resistant to diseases. Flower arrangers delight in this variety as the blooms last well when cut and displayed. In some catalogues it is listed as a Grandiflora. Few roses have received as many awards as this outstanding variety.

'Pink Parfait'

'Queen Elizabeth'

'Rosemary Rose'

'Red Gold'

'Sarabande'

'Satchmo'

'Scented Air'

'Red Gold'

Height: 75cm (2.5ft)
Spread: 60cm (2ft)
Also spelled 'Redgold', this Floribunda was introduced in 1967 and is now very popular, receiving acclaim in both North America and Europe. Its parentage includes 'Karl Herbst', 'Masquerade', 'Faust' and 'Piccadilly'. It has a fiery appearance, with red on the petal edges and gold in the interior. It is at its most attractive when the flowers first open, as with age the colours merge and fade to an overall light orange. The medium green, semi-glossy foliage creates a background for the blooms. When cut, flowers are long lasting.

'Rosemary Rose'

Height: 75cm (2.5ft)
Spread: 60–75cm (2–2.5ft)
This distinctive rose was introduced in 1955, from a cross between an unnamed seedling and 'Gruss an Templitz'. It develops superb flowers with a camellia appearance that are borne in large trusses. The blooms are bright carmine, with a slight fragrance. The vigorous, branching shoots bear medium green, purplish, matt leaves that are susceptible to mildew, rust and black spot disease.

'Sarabande'

Height: 75–90cm (2.5–3ft)
Spread: 75cm (2.5ft)
This 1957 introduction resulted from a cross between 'Cocorico' and 'Moulin Rouge'. It forms a compact plant, ideal for planting in a small rose bed. Single, bright scarlet flowers, that open to reveal cushions of golden stamens, are borne in large trusses on freely branching stems.

'Satchmo'

Height: 75cm (2.5ft)
Spread: 60–75cm (2–2.5ft)
This distinctive rose was introduced in 1970 from a cross between 'Evelyn Fison' and 'Diamant'. It produces closely packed trusses of bright but dark vermilion, loosely double, petal-packed flowers with some scent. They have the superb quality of retaining their intense colour to a late stage, thereby creating a wonderful impact of colour. Plants are bushy and compact, with dark green leaves. It is ideal for planting in beds in a garden.

'Scented Air'

Height: 90cm (3ft)
Spread: 75–90cm (2.5–3ft)
As its name suggests, this rose is known for fragrance, saturating the air with a pronounced fruity bouquet. It was introduced in 1965 from a cross between a seedling of 'Spartan' and 'Queen Elizabeth' and has proved to be free-flowering, with a repeat-flowering nature. The deep salmon-pink flowers are moderately packed with petals, expanding to 7.5cm (3in) wide when open. Plants are vigorous, with bushy growth and glossy leaves.

'Sea Pearl'
Height: 90–100cm (3–3.5ft)
Spread: 90cm (3ft)
Also known as 'Flower Girl' and raised from a cross between 'Perfecta' and 'Montezuma', this 1964 introduction has Hybrid Tea-shaped flowers when young. Blooms are slightly fragrant, pink with a yellow reverse, and with age lose their pointed shape. The shoots are vigorous and upright, carrying attractive, medium green, glossy leaves. Take care not to plant rose beds completely massed with this variety, as, apart from being repetitive once the first flush of roses is over, there is often a gap before further blooms appear.

The Times Rose
Height: 75–90cm (2.5–3ft)
Spread: 75cm (2.5ft)
Also known as 'Korpeahn' and raised from a cross between 'Tornado' and 'Red Gold', this superb rose has been acknowledged by several awards. The petal-packed, scented, large flowers have blood-red petals and are borne in large clusters. These are enhanced by the dark green leaves that are bronze-tinted when young.

'Trumpeter'
Height: 50cm (20in)
Spread: 45–50cm (18–20in)
Also known as 'Mactru', this compact, bushy and low-growing variety has petal-packed, bright vermilion, slightly fragrant flowers. It was raised from a cross between 'Satchmo' and an unnamed seedling. The leaves are dark green and glossy, and very resistant to diseases. The flowers, however, tend to become weighed down by rain.

'White Pet'
Height: 60–90cm (2–3ft)
Spread: 60–75cm (2–2.5ft)
This rose was introduced in 1879, and through its Polyantha parentage it is frequently listed as a shrub rose. It is well worthy of inclusion in a garden, whatever its classification. It is also known as 'Little White Pet' when it is a Miniature.

Other recommended Floribunda Roses:

'All Gold'	'Fashion'	'Nicole'
'Angel Face'	'French Lace'	'Orange Wave'
'Australian Gold'	'Gentle Touch'	'Pink Bountiful'
'Betty Prior'	'Glenfiddich'	'Red Hot'
'Blessings'	'Greensleeves'	'Royal Occasion'
'Chinatown'	'Hedgefire'	'Seaspray'
'Class Act'	'Ice White'	'Shepherdess'
'Copper Pot'	'Langford Light'	'Showy Gold'
'Dearest'	'Lavender Dream'	'Spartan'
'Dorothy Wheatcroft'	'Natali'	'Valentine'

'Sea Pearl'

'The Times Rose'

'Trumpeter'

'White Pet'

'Young Venturer'

'Yvonne Rabier'

This is an indication of its variable and relative small stature. It creates large clusters of small, fully double, fragrant, pompon-like white flowers throughout summer. The blooms are borne amid an abundance of dark green leaves. It is a rose with great 'old-world' charm.

'Young Venturer'
Height: 90cm (3ft)
Spread: 75–90cm (2.5–3ft)
Also known as 'Mattsun', and raised from a cross between 'Arthur Bell' and 'Cynthia Brooke', this Floribunda Rose was introduced in 1979. It creates a wealth of beautiful flowers, apricot blended with soft orange and gold. An attractive feast of colour can be achieved by planting these roses in a garden bed. It also has good scent.

'Yvonne Rabier'
Height: 1–1.2m (3–4ft)
Spread: 90cm (3ft)
Introduced in 1910 from a cross between *Rosa wichuraiana* and a white Polyantha, this rose forms a very vigorous bush. Small, petal-packed and rosette-shaped, white flowers with small petals are borne freely in medium-sized trusses. The flowers have the bonus of being sweetly scented. The growth is strong, with small, dark green, glossy leaves. Take care not to prune it severely, as this encourages growth rather than more flowers.

Climbers & Ramblers

Climbers and Ramblers are superb for clothing walls and fences, as well as pergolas, pillars and rustic screens. The essential difference between them is that Climbers create a permanent framework of stiff stems and bear their flowers on side shoots produced during the year, while Ramblers have long, vigorous and pliable stems that mostly grow from ground level.

These roses vary enormously in their vigour, so ensure that the plant of your choice suits the area available. The height is indicated for each plant, but this may vary slightly depending on the soil and climate. Also, the height and shape are invariably influenced by the supporting structure and the space allotted.

'Albéric Barbier'

'Albertine'

'Alchymist'

'Altissimo'

'Albéric Barbier'
Height: 6–7.5m (20–25ft)
This well-established and world-famous Rambler was introduced in 1900 from a cross between *Rosa wichuraiana* and 'Shirley Hibberd'. It is ideal for growing on a pillar or arch, and is especially useful to form a screen.

The yellow buds open to reveal fragrant, fully double, creamy white flowers, often 7.5cm (3in) wide, in small clusters during midsummer. After the first flush this vigorous rose produces a good second display; the plant is seldom without flowers until autumn. The almost evergreen, abundant foliage is dark green and glossy.

'Albertine'
Height: 4.5–6m (15–20ft)
This is perhaps the best known Rambler, introduced in 1921 from a cross between *Rosa wichuraiana* and 'Mrs A. R. Waddell'. It is ideal for planting against walls, forming screens and covering arches. It can also be encouraged to grow into trees. The reddish salmon buds open quickly to reveal sweetly fragrant, almost double, coppery pink flowers in early summer. The foliage is dark green and matt, reddish when young, but susceptible to mildew. Also, the blooms are often damaged by heavy rain showers.

'Alchymist'
Height: 1.8–2.4m (6–8ft)
Introduced in 1956 as a Modern Shrub Rose, when it can grow as much as 1.8m (6ft) high and 1.5m (5ft) wide, it is also often grown as a Climber. The large, full, and rosette-shaped flowers are golden yellow and flushed with orange. The whole rose has a pleasantly old appearance and flowers intermittently throughout the summer season. The name of this rose is also seen spelled 'Alchemist'.

'American Pillar'

'Bantry Bay'

'Altissimo'
Height: 2.4–3m (8–10ft)
This short Climber, introduced in 1966, has large, single, blood-red flowers shaded with crimson. Each flower is 10–13cm (4–5in) wide. The flowers are borne in small trusses, repeatedly throughout summer and into autumn. It may need protection from black spot.

'American Pillar'
Height: 4.5–6m (15–20ft)
Introduced in 1902 from a cross between *Rosa wichuraiana*, *Rosa setigera*, and a red Hybrid Perpetual, this Ramber has slowly lost overall acclaim from rosarians, but is still worth growing. The small, single, deep pink flowers have white eyes and are borne in large trusses in midsummer. Regrettably, the flowers are not scented. The dark green, glossy foliage needs regular spraying against mildew.

'Bantry Bay'
Height: 3m (10ft)
This delicately coloured, large-flowered Climber was introduced in 1967 from a cross between 'New Dawn' and 'Korona'. The slightly fragrant, semi-double, rose-pink flowers with a tinge of salmon have deeper shadings at their centres. The shapely, 7.5cm (3in) wide flowers open flat and appear throughout summer, amid medium green, semi-glossy, vigorous foliage.

'Bobby James'
Height: 7.5m (25ft)
A vigorous Rambler, this rose was introduced in 1960. It is ideal for growing to climb into trees. During midsummer it bears semi-double, six- or seven-petalled, ivory white flowers in large trusses. When in bud they are creamy, with fully open flowers revealing attractive bright yellow stamens. This rose is well known for its strong scent.

The long stems are pliable and adorned with masses of green leaves. It can form a dense canopy of flowers and foliage.

'Cécile Brunner, Climbing'
Height: 6m (20ft)
The ordinary 'Cécile Brunner' is a delightfully dainty, small shrub rose. Its climbing form, however, is vigorous, reaching 6m (20ft) and spreading to a similar distance. Its double flowers are small, shell-pink and slightly fragrant. However, unlike its smaller counterpart, it bears its flowers mainly in early summer, with only light repeat-flowering later in the year. The foliage is dark green and resistant to diseases. This climbing form originated in California.

'Compassion'
Height: 2.4m (8ft)
Introduced in 1973, this large-flowered Climber has become increasingly popular, displaying highly fragrant, salmon-pink

'Bobby James'

'Cécile Brunner, Climbing'

'Compassion'

'Crimson Shower'

'Crimson Glory, Climbing'

'Danse du Feu'

'Dorothy Perkins'

flowers which are flushed with apricot-orange as they open. Flowering is throughout summer. The dark green leaves create a pleasant foil for the flowers. For a colour contrast, position it against a white wall. Alternatively, plant it to climb a pillar near a path, where the fragrance can be readily appreciated.

'Crimson Glory, Climbing'
Height: 3–4.5m (10–15ft)
Introduced in 1946 as a sport from the Hybrid Tea 'Crimson Glory', this rose has established itself as a favourite in both Britain and North America. The double, large, richly scented, deep crimson flowers eventually assume purple tints. As the flowers open they have a loose cup-shape. It bears most of its flowers in early summer, with occasional flowers appearing later. The reddish green, semi-glossy leaves need to be sprayed regularly against mildew. It is best when planted against a wall or to climb a pillar.

'Crimson Shower'
Height: 3.5–4.5m (12–15ft)
This beautiful Rambler was introduced in 1951 and is thought to be the best variety of its colour. The small, semi-double, bright crimson flowers are shaped like rosettes and appear in midsummer and continue into autumn. The foliage creates an attractive foil for the flowers. It is an ideal variety to plant to cover an arch or to climb a pillar. It is becoming increasingly popular because of its unfading flowers and its ability to carry on flowering after the main flush is over.

'Danse du Feu'
Height: 2.4–3m (8–10ft)
Also known as 'Spectacular', this rose was introduced in 1954 from a cross between 'Paul's Scarlet Climber' and a *Rosa multiflora* seedling. It was one of the first modern repeat-flowering Climbers. The scentless, semi-double, brilliant orange-scarlet flowers become rather globular, and are borne in moderately sized trusses. Unfortunately, with age, the flowers become purple. Flowering is throughout summer and well into autumn. The medium green foliage, bronze-tinted when young, is glossy and creates an interesting background for the flowers.

'Dorothy Perkins'
Height: 4.5m (15ft)
This old and well-established Rambler was introduced in 1901 from a cross between *Rosa wichuraiana* and 'Madame Gabriel Luizet', and it is still popular today. The scentless, double, rose-pink flowers are small and rosette in shape, and borne in large trusses during late summer. The growth is rampant and formed of medium green, glossy leaves that usually need regular spraying against mildew.

'Dortmund'
Height: 2.4–3m (8–10ft)
A repeat-flowering Climber, this rose was introduced in 1955 from a cross between a seedling and *Rosa kordesii*. The scentless, single, large flowers are bright red with a white eye and a central boss of yellow stamens. They are borne in large trusses throughout summer and into autumn. The foliage is dark green and glossy. It is best when planted to grow up a pillar.

'Dreaming Spires'
Height: 3–4.5m (10–15ft)
This bright, repeat-flowering Climber has sparkling golden yellow flowers. The blooms have a distinct fragrance and appear amid heavy, dark green leaves. They are borne on attractive, vigorous, upright growths. It is pleasantly attractive throughout the summer.

'Emily Gray'
Height: 3.5–4.5m (12–15ft)
This Rambler was introduced at the end of the First World War, in 1918. It resulted from a cross between 'Jersey Beauty' and 'Comtesse du Cayla' and produces uniquely coloured, semi-double, fragrant, midsummer flowers. The flowers are a rich golden buff with a deeper colouring at the centre. When in bud, they are high and pointed, but will open to create flat flowers borne in small trusses. The dark green, glossy leaves, bronze when young, are almost evergreen and borne on purplish crimson shoots. Its evergreen tendency makes it ideal for planting to cover an arch or to create a screen. Only very light pruning is needed; excessive pruning encourages too much growth.

'Etoile de Hollande, Climbing'
Height: 3.5–5.4m (12–18ft)
This climbing rose was introduced in 1931 as a sport from the Hybrid Tea of the same name. It is vigorous, with strongly fragrant, double, but loosely formed, deep velvety crimson flowers. Flowers mainly appear in midsummer, with uncertain subsequent flushes in late summer and early autumn. The abundantly borne, dark green foliage is semi-glossy and creates an attractive foil for the flowers. It is ideal for planting against a wall, and useful for introducing scent into a garden.

'François Juranville'
Height: 6–7.5m (20–25ft)
This old and established Rambler was introduced in 1906 from a cross between *Rosa wichuraiana* and 'Madame Laurette Messimy' It is very vigorous, bearing flat, small-petalled, double flowers of a glowing pink tinted with gold towards their centres. The flowers have the bonus of a sweetbriar fragrance. Flowering occurs during early summer. The small,

'Dortmund'

'Dreaming Spires'

'Emily Gray'

'François Juranville'

'Etoile de Hollande, Climbing'

'Galway Bay'

'Golden Showers'

dark green and glossy leaves are reddish bronze when young. The stems are long and flexible. This rose is best not planted against walls, as the decreased air circulation makes it prone to mildew.

'Galway Bay'
Height: 2.4m (8ft)
This 1966 introduction has 'Queen Elizabeth' and 'Heidelberg' in its parentage and creates a large-flowered Climber, ideal for planting to grow up a pillar. The large, semi-double, slightly fragrant, medium pink flowers are a deeper colour towards the edges of the petals. They are borne in clusters throughout summer and into autumn. The leaves are medium green.

'Golden Showers'
Height: 2.4–3m (8–10ft)
A very popular large-flowered Climber, 'Golden Showers' was introduced in 1956 from a cross between 'Charlotte Armstrong' and 'Captain Thomas'. The resulting semi-double, fragrant, golden yellow flowers with pointed buds have been widely acclaimed by many rosarians. However, the flowers fade with age. Flowering extends from early summer until the frosts of autumn. The blooms are carried on vigorous, upright growths also bearing dark green, bronze-tinted, glossy leaves, which often need regular spraying against black spot.

'Guinée'
Height: 4.5m (15ft)
This extremely well-known, large-flowered Climber was introduced in 1938 from a cross between 'Souvenir de Claudius Denoyel' and 'Ami Quinard'. The highly fragrant, rich, dark, velvety crimson flowers open to about 10cm (4in) wide. They are unfading and have bright golden stamens at their centres. Flowering is in early summer. The foliage is medium green and semi-glossy, and susceptible to mildew. It is ideal for planting to cover walls or pillars. Additionally, it can be used as support for other weak-stemmed climbing plants such as honeysuckle and *Clematis viticella*.

'Handel'
Height: 3m (10ft)
'Handel' is an eye-catching, large-flowered Climber which originated in 1965. It was raised from a cross between 'Columbine' and 'Heidelberg'. The shapely buds open to reveal cream-coloured, slightly fragrant flowers flushed pink and edged in deep pink. Flowering continues over a long period. The foliage is dark green, glossy and tinted bronze. It is best when planted to climb a pillar. Spraying against mildew may be necessary.

'Iceberg, Climbing'
Height: 3m (10ft)
This Climber was introduced in 1968, as a sport of the well-known and

'Guinée'

'Handel'

'Iceberg, Climbing'

'Joseph's Coat'

'Lady Hillingdon, Climbing'

'Madame Alfred Carrière'

'Madame Grégoire Staechelin'

highly popular Floribunda of the same name. The double, white, slightly fragrant flowers appear throughout summer and continue into autumn. They are borne amid medium green, glossy leaves that soon smother a wall. Be prepared to spray against mildew.

'Joseph's Coat'
Height: 3m (10ft)
Introduced in 1964 from a cross between 'Buccaneer' and 'Circus', this rose creates a large-flowered Climber with colourful flowers. The blooms are moderately full, golden yellow, heavily flushed and overlaid with orange-flame and cherry-red. They are produced throughout much of the summer and borne in medium trusses. The medium green, semi-glossy foliage creates a superb background for the flowers. It can be planted as a specimen rose in a shrub border, or to climb a pillar.

'Lady Hillingdon, Climbing'
Height: 4.5m (15ft)
This superb and very reliable rose is best when planted against a warm wall facing the sun, but is successful in most aspects. The rich, apricot-yellow flowers are lax and elegant, and reveal a rich Tea rose bouquet. Flowering is throughout summer. The luxuriant foliage is dark green and helps to smother unsightly walls.

This Climber is a sport from the 1910 introduction 'Lady Hillingdon', which was raised at Lowe and Shawyers in England, at one time the largest glasshouse nursery in the world.

'Madame Alfred Carrière'
Height: 6m (20ft)
This very old and well-established Noisette Climber was introduced in 1879 and has been popular ever since. It is a strong-growing rose that bears sweetly scented, large, cupped, white flowers with a flesh-pink tinge. The flowers are borne throughout summer and into autumn. Its ability to grow vigorously and reliably on a shaded wall has made it especially useful in gardens. The foliage is light green.

'Madame Grégoire Staechelin'
Height: 6m (20ft)
Also known as 'Spanish Beauty' and introduced in 1927, this large-flowered Climber has been popular for many years. The cupped, glowing pink flowers are lightly shaded crimson and have the scent of sweet peas. Clusters of them are borne in early summer, amid medium green leaves. It is superb when planted to cover a wall. The attractive hips can be left for decorating homes during winter holidays. Even though the flowers appear only once in a season, it is magnificent.

'Mermaid'
Height: 7.5m (25ft)
One of the best known large-flowered Climbers, this rose was introduced in 1918 from a cross between *Rosa bracteata* and a Tea rose. The fragrant, primrose-yellow flowers, often 10cm (4in) wide, have amber-coloured stamens and appear repeatedly throughout summer and even until late autumn and early winter, if the weather is not too severe and the position is sheltered. The flowers are borne in clusters amid medium green, glossy leaves that have a bronze tinge. Unfortunately, the stems are brittle and thorny, and need to be handled carefully to avoid breakage.

It is a rose that often takes two years to become established and is best planted against a warm wall facing the sun. It is vigorous, and often needs frequent attention to tie in new growths before they obstruct paths. Since its introduction it has become one of the most popular Climbers, and well deserves a place in every rose garden.

'Parade'
Height: 3m (10ft)
Introduced in 1953, this relatively new rose has a pleasingly old-fashioned appearance that appeals to many rosarians. It originated from a cross between a seeding of 'New Dawn' and 'World's Fair'. The many-petalled flowers are highly scented, deep carmine-pink and borne in large clusters, mainly in midsummer, but with slight repeats later in the summer. The dark green, glossy foliage is disease-resistant, and tinged red when young. Plant it to climb a pillar. It is a tough and reliable rose.

'Parkdirektor Riggers'
Height: 3.5m (12ft)
Originating from a cross between *Rosa kordesii* and 'Our Princess', this unforgettably named Climber bears large clusters of slightly fragrant, semi-double and almost single, blood-red flowers recurrently throughout summer. Remember to remove dead flowers to encourage the formation of further ones.

The foliage is dark green and glossy. This rose is especially attractive when planted to climb a pillar or to form a screen where its display of blooms will be conspicuous.

'Paul's Scarlet Climber'
Height: 3m (10ft)
Introduced in 1916 from a cross between 'Paul's Carmine Pillar' and 'Soleil d'Or', this Rambler has been popular for many years. The rounded, semi-double, scentless, deep scarlet flowers are unfading and borne in small clusters in early summer. The medium green leaves are small and glossy, and may need to be sprayed against mildew. Plant it to climb an arch or pillar, or to form a screen.

'Mermaid'

'Parade'

'Schoolgirl'

'Parkdirektor Riggers'

'Souvenir de Claudius Denoyel'

'Paul's Scarlet Climber'

'Summer Wine'

'Schoolgirl'
Height: 3m (10ft)
This large-flowered Climber was introduced in 1964 from a cross between 'Coral Dawn' and 'Belle Blonde', and has become increasingly popular. The slightly fragrant, Hybrid Tea-shaped flowers are orange-apricot and fade to salmon-pink. The blooms appear throughout summer and into autumn. The dark green, glossy leaves are borne on vigorous stems.

'Souvenir de Claudius Denoyel'
Height: 5.4–6m (18–20ft)
This vigorous Climber was introduced in 1920 from a cross between 'Château de Clos Vougeot' and 'Commandeur Jules Gravereaux'. The bright, richly fragrant, cupped, crimson-red, large and semi-double, unfading flowers are borne intermittently throughout the season, but mostly during early summer and midsummer. It is well worth including in a scented rose garden.

'Summer Wine'
Height: 3–4.5m (10–15ft)
A repeat-flowering type, this Climber reveals attractive, single, very fragrant, coral-pink flowers which are highlighted by prominent red stamens. The exquisite pink flowers will exhibit a good display throughout the summer season. It is a vigorous climbing rose, with deep green foliage.

'Swan Lake'

Height: 2.4m (8ft)

A free-flowering Climber, this rose was introduced in 1968 and bears large, beautifully formed and fully double white flowers with pink undertones in their centres. It grows strongly, with the benefit of Hybrid Tea-type flowers.

'Sympathie'

Height: 3m (10ft)

This large-flowered Climber was introduced in 1964. The sweetly scented, moderately full and medium-sized, velvety crimson flowers have a Hybrid Tea appearance and emerge in midsummer, with repeat-flowering occurring later. They are carried in medium-sized clusters. The leaves are dark green and glossy. Plant this climbing rose to grow up and around a pillar.

'The Garland'

Height: 4.5m (15ft)

This beautiful Rambler was introduced in 1835 and was said to be a cross between *Rosa moschata* and *Rosa multiflora*. During midsummer it reveals bunches of small, creamy salmon, fairly double flowers, fading to white. The narrow, quilled petals create an attractive daisy-like appearance. It is also known for its richly orange-scented flowers. The flowers are borne on erect stalks, and it is an ideal rose for planting to cover a wall or an arch; the roses appear among bushy and twiggy growth. In

'Swan Lake'

'Sympathie'

'Wedding Day'

'The Garland'

'White Cockade'

'Zéphirine Drouhin'

autumn it has the bonus of bearing small, oval, red hips. Other attractive qualities are its green wood and purplish brown prickles. It can be grown as a shrub in a border, but is more eye-catching when planted to cover a wall.

'Wedding Day'
Height: 7.5–9m (25–30ft)
A prolific and vigorous Rambler introduced in 1950, this rose bears fragrant, eye-catching, five-petalled, single, cream-coloured flowers in huge clusters during midsummer. Unfortunately, the flowers lose their colour and turn white. The foliage is medium green. The whole plant is ideal for covering large walls or for growing to clamber into trees. Avoid planting it in very wet areas, as the petals become spotted pink after heavy storms.

'White Cockade'
Height: 2.4m (8ft)
A beautiful large-flowered Climber, 'White Cockade' has slightly fragrant, double, white flowers that appear over many months. The foliage is medium green and glossy, and resistant to diseases. It can be grown as a large plant in a shrub border or, preferably, to climb a pillar.

'Zephirine Drouhin'
Height: 3–3.5m (10–12ft)
Also known as the 'Thornless Rose', this rose has become one of the best-known Climbers. It was introduced in 1868, and is of Bourbon descent. The fragrant, semi-double, deep rose-pink flowers are produced throughout summer, especially if the dead flowers are regularly removed. Its massed and continuous display of flowers gives this remarkable Climber its fame. The leaves are light green, matt and tinted red, and usually need to be sprayed against mildew. It is ideal for growing against walls, even a shaded one. It is also superb in a shrub border or for forming into a hedge. Indeed, it is one of the rose world's most reliable Climbers.

Other recommended Climbers & Ramblers:

'Adeläide d'Orléans (Rambler)	'Lawrence Johnston' (Climber)
'Allen Chandler' (Climber)	'Maigold' (Climber)
'America' (Climber)	'May Queen' (Rambler)
'Blaze' (Climber)	'New Dawn' (Climber)
'Bleu Magenta' (Rambler)	'Paul's Lemon Pillar' (Climber)
'Céline Forestier' (Climber)	'Pink Perpetue' (Climber)
'Don Juan' (Climber)	'René André' (Rambler)
'Francis E. Lester' (Rambler)	'Sander's White' (Rambler)
'Gloire de Dijon' (Climber)	'Silver Moon' (Rambler)
'Goldfinch' (Rambler)	'Veilchenblau' (Rambler)

Miniature Roses

These are hardy, deciduous shrubs, with all the charm and beauty of their larger counterparts, but a great deal smaller. The branching stems are almost thornless and bear miniature flowers. Heights vary, some growing 30–45cm (12–18in) high, while others are less than 15cm (6in). In recent years, more miniature varieties have been introduced, many ideal for window-boxes and troughs, edges to borders and on the smallest of patios. Avoid positioning them in troughs on top of high walls, as they are best seen from above, and not from the side. Miniatures must always be grown from cuttings, as those that are budded soon lose their dwarf characteristic.

'Angela Rippon'
Height: 30cm (12in)
Also known as 'Ocaru' and 'Ocarina' and introduced in 1978 from a cross between 'Rosy Jewel' and 'Zorina', this is a well-known Miniature Rose that creates a compact yet bushy plant. It is suited to be grown in small rose beds. The flowers are double, pale carmine-pink and borne freely. Additionally, they are fragrant and ideal for positioning near a window.

'Baby Darling'
Height: 20–30cm (8–12in)
This rose was introduced during 1964 from a cross between 'Little Darling' and 'Magic Wand'. It is dwarf and bushy, with beautiful, double, salmon-orange flowers. It is a rose that does not appear to be susceptible to mildew. All collections of Miniature Roses should have this daintily pretty variety, which was raised in California.

'Baby Masquerade'
Height: 30–38cm (12–15in)
This rose is attractive, with double, slightly fragrant, Floribunda-type flowers that change from yellow to pink, and then to red. Flowering is mainly during early summer and midsummer, on strong and easily grown plants. It was raised in 1956 from a cross between 'Tom Thumb' and 'Masquerade', and is often known as 'Baby Carnival'. Compared with some Miniatures, it is tall and bushy, superb for a position where a small but dominant feature is needed.

It is especially suited as a cut flower, the buds being only the size of a thimble.

'Baby Sunrise'
Height: 20–25cm (8–10in)
Also known as 'Macparlez' and introduced in 1984, this rose's parentage has not been revealed. However, its attractive, soft peach flowers are borne amid medium green, disease-resistant,

'Angela Rippon'

'Baby Darling'

'Baby Masquerade'

'Chelsea Pensioner'

'Baby Sunrise'

'Cinderella'

glossy leaves. It is ideal for planting in containers, such as window-boxes.

'Chelsea Pensioner'
Height: 30–38cm (12–15in)
Also known as 'Mattche' and introduced in 1982 from a cross between a seedling of 'Gold Pin' and an unnamed seedling, this rose has proved to be very attractive. The dark red flowers, with faintly golden yellow central parts, are borne on slightly lax but relatively stiff stems that display dark green, shiny leaves.

'Cinderella'
Height: 15–23cm (6–9in)
This fascinating Miniature Rose was introduced in 1952 from a cross between 'Cécile Brunner' and 'Tom Thumb'. It has small, scented, white flowers packed with petals, somewhat resembling in shape those of Hybrid Teas.

Flowers are further highlighted with dark shades of pink, and appear amid dark, shiny leaves on stiff and upright, thornless stems. Flower arrangers admire this rose, as the blooms last a long time when cut and placed in water. This pretty rose is also suitable for using as a standard.

Although some rosarians advocate underfeeding this Miniature to ensure that the growth remains small, it is just as attractive when fed properly, creating a plant that is healthier and more resistant to diseases.

'Colibri'

Height: 20–25cm (8–10in)
A bushy Miniature Rose with double, bright red-orange flowers borne in clusters amid attractive and glossy leaves. It was introduced in 1959 from a cross between 'Goldilocks' and 'Perla de Montserrat'. Unfortunately, it is susceptible to black spot disease.

'Colibri 79' was introduced quite a few years later, and grows to about 25cm (10in) high. It produces brightly coloured, golden apricot flowers with slight pinkish shades. These plants are also bushy, and are sometimes sold as 'Meidanover'

'Darling Flame'

Height: 30cm (12in)
This well-known Miniature Rose, introduced in 1971 with 'Rimosa', 'Rosina' and 'Zambra' in its parentage, is sometimes known as 'Minuetto'. It creates a bushy and healthy plant that develops double, rich orange-vermilion flowers with attractive gold reverses. The foliage is also attractive, dark green and glossy, but care must be taken to ensure black spot does not become established. Additionally, the profusely borne flowers have a slightly fruity fragrance. It is widely grown on the European continent.

'Gold Pin'

Height: 30cm (12in)
Introduced in 1974, with unrecorded parentage, this rose develops exceptionally

'Colibri'

'Gold Pin'

'Darling Flame'

'Green Diamond'

'Lavender Jewel'

'Peek-a-Boo'

'Perle d'Alcanada'

attractive, semi-double, light gold flowers on long stems. These are highlighted by foliage that has bronze shades when young. Unfortunately, it is rather susceptible to an infection of black spot disease.

'Green Diamond'
Height: 30cm (12in)
This fascinating Miniature Rose was introduced in 1975 and bred in North America. Although not to everyone's taste, the pale lime-green, small, full and rosette-shaped flowers are eye-catching. They are tinted pink when first opening. Hot weather tends to fade the green, causing it to lose its visual impact. It was raised from a cross between an unnamed seedling and 'Sheri Anne'.

It is wise not to plant it *en masse*, as the flowers lose their impact and the display appears anaemic. Instead, use only a few plants. Flower arrangers usually find it attractive, but use it only in moderation, perhaps to highlight other flowers.

'Lavender Jewel'
Height: 30cm (12in)
This popular variety was introduced in 1978, resulting from a cross between 'Little Chief' and 'Angel Face'. The large, double, pink flowers have a lavender haze. They are slow to open and do not quickly fade. Additionally, they are freely borne on bushy but slightly lax and spreading plants.

Regrettably, the blooms are not very fragrant. Flower arrangers and exhibitors usually find it a useful miniature variety.

'Peek-a-Boo'
Height: 38–45cm (15–18in)
Also known as 'Brass Ring' and 'Dicgrow', this is a 1981 introduction with 'Bangor', 'Korbell' and 'Nozomi' in its parentage. It is sometimes classified as a patio rose. It is slightly larger than most Miniature Roses, but nevertheless has a small stance. It is compact and forms a cushion smothered with small, soft apricot flowers that open flat. These are borne in attractively graceful sprays. As well as being grown for garden display, it is frequently displayed at exhibition shows.

'Perle d'Alcanada'
Height: 20–25cm (10–12in)
Also known as 'Baby Crimson', 'Pearl of Canada', 'Titania' and 'Wheatcroft's Baby Crimson', this rose was introduced in 1944 from a cross between 'Perle des Rouges' and *Rosa rouletii*. It produces shapely buds that open to reveal semi-double, carmine flowers. The bases of the petals are white, but not obviously so. The leaves are dark and glossy, with the whole plant having a wide-spreading nature. It is a diminutive plant that deserves a place in a Miniature Rose garden.

127

'Pour Toi'
Height: 25cm (10in)
Also known as 'Para Ti', 'For You' and 'Wendy', this charming introduction from 1946 evolved from a cross between 'Eduardo Toda' and 'Pompon de Paris'. It develops small, semi-double, white flowers with a creamy white shading. The blooms are borne on long stems, and are well able to withstand bad weather which often harms white varieties. Plants are bushy, with the slightly scented flowers profusely borne amid the green and glossy leaves.

It is a well-established rose that has been grown for many years and is ideal for planting in troughs and rock gardens.

'Rosina'
Height: 25–38cm (10–15in)
Also known as 'Josephine Wheatcroft', this Miniature is the result of a cross between *Rosa rouletii* and 'Eduardo Toda', and was introduced in 1951. The crossing has produced a beautiful Hybrid Tea-type Miniature Rose. It develops eye-catching, bright yellow, double flowers borne throughout summer, with about ten blooms in each truss. Each flower is beautifully formed and slightly fragrant, as well as tapering, and borne amid green, glossy leaves, making them ideal for buttonholes and decorating tables.

'Royal Salute'
Height: 38cm (15in)
This beautiful and dainty Miniature Rose has sweetly scented, rose-pink flowers. The blooms are borne on very bushy plants. This rose is ideal for planting alongside a path where it will be noticed and its fragrance enjoyed.

'Snow Ball'
Height: 25cm (10in)
This delightful Miniature Rose well deserves its name, which is also spelled 'Snowball'. Very small, rounded, white flowers in clustered heads appear above the dark green leaves. Unfortunately, it is not scented. It was introduced in 1984 from unrecorded parents. Nevertheless, it has become a very popular rose.

'Pour Toi'

'Rosina'

'Royal Salute'

'Snow Ball'

Other recommended Miniature Roses:

'Anytime'	'Dresden Doll'	'New Penny'
'Baby Betsy McCall'	'Easter Morning'	'Pink Sunblaze'
'Baby Goldstar'	'Galaxy'	'Robin Red Breast'
'Baby Katie'	'Honest Abe'	'Sheri Anne'
'Bambino'	'Innocent Blush'	'Stars 'n Stripes'
'California Sun'	'Little Eskimo'	'White Angel'
'Coralin'	'Little Flirt'	'Yorkshire Sunblaze'

'Starina'

'Sweet Fairy'

'Starina'
Height: 25cm (10 in)

This rose is an introduction from 1965, and has 'Dany Robin', 'Fire King' and 'Perla de Montserrat' in its parentage. It is also known as 'Meigabi', and is one of the best Miniature Roses, having proved itself over many years. The flowers are shapely, well-formed, rich orange-scarlet and freely borne from early summer to late autumn or even into early winter if the weather is mild. The whole plant is vigorous, with glossy leaves.

It has many purposes, from being planted in a bed alongside a patio to setting in troughs, window-boxes and pots. Additionally, when cut, the beautiful flowers are long-lasting. It has also been grown as a standard.

'Sweet Fairy'
Height: 20–25cm (8–10in)

This attractive Miniature has well-formed, superbly scented, lilac-pink flowers, about 2.5cm (1in) wide and bursting with approximately sixty petals. It was introduced in 1946 from a cross between 'Tom Thumb' and an unnamed seedling. It is further enhanced by dark green leaves. Widely used by flower arrangers, it is particularly ideal for creating a diminutive display for small tables.

As with other Miniatures, this rose looks best positioned in a rose bed with others of its same stature. It may help to plant it in slightly raised beds.

Species Roses

Species Roses include wild roses from many parts of the world, together with their natural and man-made hybrids. Most are hardy shrubs, have attractive foliage, and single flowers with five petals, although some of the hybrids have semi-double or double flowers. Many have highly scented flowers and develop attractively shaped and colourful hips in autumn. Most species form shrubs, some with a ground-covering habit. A few, however, are very vigorous Climbers.

Rosa banksiae 'Lutea'

Rosa banksiae

Height: 6m (20ft) or more
Spread: 2.4–3m (8–10ft)
Rosa banksiae is a vigorous rose from Central and West China. It is known as Banks' Rose and Lady Banks' Rose. During early summer it bears sweetly scented, double, white flowers, 2.5cm (1in) wide. These are followed by small, round red hips. Several forms are grown: *R. b. lutescens* with yellow and single flowers; 'Lutea', the Yellow Banksian, with double, yellow, rosette-like flowers; and *R. b. normalis* with creamy white flowers.

Rosa californica

Height: 1.8–2.1m (6–7ft)
Spread: 1.2–1.8m (4–6ft)
A stoutly prickled shrub from the western states of America, *R. californica* bears 4cm (1.5in) wide, carmine-pink flowers from early summer. Round, red hips follow. This rose is mostly grown in the form *R.c. plena*, which has sweetly scented, semi-double, deep pink flowers on pendulous stems.

Rosa centifolia

Height: 90cm–1.5m (3–5ft)
Spread: 90cm–1.5m (3–5ft)
This prickly stemmed shrub has fragrant leaves and scented, 7.5cm (3in) wide, double, flat-topped, pink flowers during midsummer. It is known as the Cabbage Rose, Provence Rose and Holland Rose. It is usually grown in its many forms, such as: 'Bullata', which has crinkly, lettuce-like leaves; 'Muscosa', called the Common Moss Rose, which has resin-scented glands and richly scented, clear pink, double flowers; and 'Parviflora', the Burgundian Rose or Burgundinaca, which has small, flat, deep rose flowers suffused with claret.

Rosa damascena

Height 1.8m (6ft)
Spread: 1.8m (6ft)
This is called the Damask Rose and is a grey-leaved shrub from western Asia with 7.5cm (3in) wide, double, fragrant flowers, varying in colour from white to red. These are followed by bristly, red hips. It is often grown in the form

Rosa californica plena

Rosa centifolia

Rosa damascena 'Versicolor'

Rosa foetida bicolor

Rosa gallica 'Versicolor'

'Versicolor' (York and Lancaster) which has semi-double, white, pink or bicoloured flowers.

Rosa foetida
Height: 1.5m (5ft)
Spread: 1.2–1.5m (4–5ft)
This is known as Austrian Briar and Austrian Yellow. It is a small, suckering shrub from western Asia with 5–6cm (2–2.5in) wide, bright buttercup-yellow flowers. There are two interesting forms: *R.f. bicolor*, the Austrian Copper, with copper-red on the inner sides and yellow on the reverses; and 'Persiana', the Persian Yellow, with golden yellow, double flowers.

Rosa gallica
Height: 90cm (3ft)
Spread: 90cm (3ft)
Rosa gallica has many names: French Rose, Provins Rose and the Rose of Provins. It is a small, suckering rose from southern Europe and western Asia and develops deep pink solitary flowers, 5–7.5cm (2–3in) wide, followed by red, round or top-shaped hips. It is invariably grown as: 'Complicata' which has single, pink flowers; 'Officinalis', the Apothecary's Rose, which has fragrant, semi-double, rosy crimson flowers; and 'Versicolor', also known as 'Rosa Mundi', which is a sport of 'Officinalis' and bears crimson flowers streaked with white.

Rosa hugonis

Height: 2.1m (7ft)
Spread: 1.8m (6ft)
A graceful and well-branched shrub from Central China, *R. hugonis* has 5cm (2in) wide, solitary, creamy yellow, saucer-shaped flowers with crinkly petals, appearing in early summer. They are followed in late summer by mahogany red, round hips. At the peak of its flowering season, the stems are bursting with colour.

Rosa moyesii

Height: 3–3.5m (10–12ft)
Spread: 2.4–3m (8–10ft)
A well-known shrub from western China, *R. moyesii* creates a wealth of rich, blood red, single flowers, 5–7.5cm (2–3in) wide, in early summer. These are followed by large, crimson, flagon-shaped hips. There are several superb forms, including: 'Geranium', with brilliant red flowers; 'Highdownensis', with cerise-crimson flowers; 'Sealing Wax', a beautiful form of *R. m. rosea*, which has vivid pink flowers; and 'Fred Streeter', a form of *R. m. rosea*, which has rich, cerise-pink flowers.

Rosa pimpinellifolia

(Rosa spinosissima)
Height: 60–90cm (2–3ft)
Spread: 60–120 cm (2–4ft)
Famously known as the Burnet Rose, Scotch Rose or The Scottish Rose, this rose is native to Europe, western Asia and the British Isles. This bristly shrub is thicket-

Rosa hugonis

Rosa moyesii 'Geranium'

Rosa rubiginosa

Rosa pimpinellifolia hispida

forming and develops solitary white or pale pink flowers during early summer. Invariably it is grown as: *R. p. altaica*, with large, single, creamy white, semi-double flowers; 'Double Yellow', also known as Prince Charles Rose, with double, deep yellow, heavily scented flowers; 'Double White', with double white flowers and a scent like lily of the valley; the yellow *R. p. hispida*; and 'Lutea', with buttercup-yellow flowers.

Rosa rubiginosa
(Rosa eglanteria)
Height: 1.8–2.4m (6–8ft)
Spread: 1.8–2.4m (6–8ft)
This shrub is popularly known as the Sweetbriar or Eglantine. It is native to Europe and Great Britain, and is noted for the strong, deliciously sweet fragrance of its foliage. In early summer it bears single, bright pink, 4cm (1.5in) wide flowers, followed later by bright red, oval hips that last well into winter.

Rosa rugosa
Height: 1.5–2.1m (5–7ft)
Spread: 1.2–1.5m (4–5ft)
This prickly and sturdy shrub is often called the Ramanas Rose or Japanese Rose. It is from North East Asia and has single, heavily scented, deep pink flowers up to 7.5cm (3in) across during early summer, then flowering intermittently until autumn. Part of its beauty is the bright red, tomato-shaped fruit. Two forms – 'Frau Dagmar Hastrup' and 'Roseraie de l'Hay' – are mentioned under Old Roses, but others include: 'Alba', with white flowers but blush-coloured when in bud; 'Rubra' with wine-crimson fragrant flowers; and 'Scabrosa', with rose-magenta, single flowers.

Rosa xanthina
Height: 1.8m (6ft)
Spread: 1.8m (6ft)
A graceful shrub from Korea and northern China, *R. xanthina* has arching stems and dainty fern-like leaves. Semi-double, golden yellow flowers about 4cm (1.5in) wide are borne in early summer and midsummer. It is mainly grown in the form 'Canary Bird', also known as *Rosa xanthina spontanea* 'Canary Bird', which has canary-yellow flowers.

Rosa rugosa 'Rubra'

Rosa xanthina 'Canary Bird'

Other recommended Species Roses:

Rosa × alba	*Rosa multiflora*
Rosa ecae	*Rosa × noisettiana*
Rosa farreri	*Rosa rubrifolia*
Rosa × harisonii	*Rosa sericea*
Rosa moschata	*Rosa wichuraiana*

Modern Shrub Roses

These hardy deciduous shrubs have a diversity of origins. Most are hybrids between Species Roses and Old Roses. They are strong and robust and make excellent shrubs for the garden, many creating colour intermittently throughout summer, others in a single but perhaps prolonged flush. Many form large shrubs, while a few are ideal for creating ground cover to smother old tree stumps or banks.

Their nature and parentage is so variable that those with a climbing nature are listed in some catalogues as Climbers.

'Aloha'

'Aloha'
Height: 1.5m (5ft)
Spread: 1.5m (5ft)
This is a beautiful rose introduced in 1949 from a cross between 'Mercedes Gallart' and 'New Dawn'. The highly fragrant, clear pink, 'old-fashioned' flowers are shaded salmon and borne repeatedly throughout summer. The foliage is medium green in colour, healthy and attractive, while the flowers are resistant to damage from rain.

'Cerise Bouquet'
Height: 2.7m (9ft)
Spread: 2.4m (8ft)
This is one of the most beautiful and graceful of Modern Shrub Roses, introduced in 1958 from a cross between *Rosa multibracteata* and 'Crimson Glory'. The raspberry-scented, semi-double, cerise-pink flowers are borne in big open sprays, and bloom intermittently throughout summer. When established, it develops arching shoots, often 3m

(10ft) long. It can also be trained into low trees.

'Constance Spry'
Height: 1.8–2.1m (6–7ft)
Spread: 1.8–2.1m (6–7ft)
This rose is a 1961 introduction. It originated from a cross between 'Belle Isis' and 'Dainty Maid' and develops magnificent, clear pink, cup-shaped flowers, resembling large paeonies. Flowering is mainly in early summer and midsummer. It has a strong myrrh fragrance and is borne amid dark green leaves that have a coppery tint when young.

It was named after Constance Spry, a great advocate of French Old Roses, which it closely resembles.

'Fritz Nobis'
Height: 1.8m (6ft)
Spread: 1.8m (6ft)
Introduced in 1940 from a cross between 'Joanna Hill' and *Rosa rubiginosa magnifica*, this rose has a bushy and arching nature. The semi-double, Hybrid

'Cerise Bouquet'

'Constance Spry'

'Fritz Nobis'

'Frühlingsgold'

'Frühlingsmorgen'

Tea-type flowers are flesh pink with darker shading. They have the bonus of a refreshing clove scent, and although flowering only once, in early summer, they create a magnificent display. The flowers are followed by reddish hips. Growth tends to zig-zag, with large prickles and attractive, glossy green leaves.

'Frühlingsgold'
Height: 2.1m (7ft)
Spread: 2.1m (7ft)
This shrub is a 1937 introduction, resulting from a cross between 'Joanna Hill' and *Rosa pimpinellifolia* 'Grandiflora'. It creates a feast of large, almost single, deliciously fragrant, sparkling, butter-yellow flowers up to 10cm (4in) wide during spring and early summer. These usually fade to creamy white, revealing yellow stamens.

'Frühlingsmorgen'
Height: 1.8m (6ft)
Spread: 1.5m (5ft)
A superb recurrent-flowering shrub, this is a 1941 introduction, with 'E. G. Hill', 'Catherine Kordes' and *Rosa pimpinellifolia* 'Grandiflora' in its parentage. It has scented, single, rose-pink flowers, up to 10cm (4in) wide, with yellow centres and purplish maroon stamens. The blooms are borne in early summer and again in late summer and early autumn. The grey-green leaves create a foil for the flowers.

'Golden Wings'
Height: 1.2–1.5m (4–5ft)
Spread: 1.2–1.5m (4–5ft)
Introduced relatively recently, in 1956, this shrub rose has become widely acclaimed. Several roses are in its immediate parentage, including 'Soeur Thérèse' and 'Ormiston Roy'. It develops large, 10cm (4in) wide, slightly scented, single, pale gold flowers with mahogany-coloured stamens. The flowers appear intermittently throughout summer. The pale green leaves create an attractive foil for the flowers.

'Nevada'
Height: 2.1m (7ft)
Spread: 2.1–2.4m (7–8ft)
This is one of the best known Modern Shrub Roses, introduced in 1927 from a cross thought to have been between the Hybrid Tea 'La Giralda' and a hybrid of *Rosa moyesii*. The semi-double, creamy white flowers, tinted pink in hot weather, are about 10cm (4in) wide, with a clear central boss of yellow stamens when fully open. They are borne along arching branches that bear light green, matt leaves.

It is a rose that needs pruning each year, and especially the removal of old and dead wood.

'Nymphenburg'
Height: 2.1–2.4m (7–8ft)
Spread: 1.8–2.1m (6–7ft)
Introduced in 1954, this shrub rose was the result of a cross between

'Golden Wings'

'Nevada'

'ymphenburg'

'carlet Fire'

'Scintillation'

'Snow Carpet'

'Sangerhausen' and 'Sunmist'. The large, sweetly apple-scented, fully double, Hybrid Tea-shaped flowers are salmon-pink and shaded cerise and orange-yellow at the base of the petals. The flowers are borne in clusters, almost continuously throughout the summer, amid glossy leaves on strong, arching stems. As well as being useful for a shrub border, it can also be grown as a Climber.

'Scarlet Fire'

Height: 2.1m (7ft)
Spread: 2.1m (7ft)
Also known as 'Scharlachglut', this 1952 introduction from a cross between 'Poinsettia' and *Rosa gallica* 'Grandiflora' has become well known for its dominant display of colour. The single, bright scarlet flowers, about 7.5cm (3in) wide, have golden stamens and are borne freely on long and arching shoots. Large pear-shaped hips follow which last well into winter and make this rose an asset in a border. Unfortunately, the flowers are borne mainly in one flush in midsummer.

'Scintillation'

Height: 1.2m (4ft)
Spread: 1.8m (6ft)
'Scintillation' is a 1968 introduction, and forms a wide-spreading shrub that is ideal for creating ground cover, whether sprawling over old tree stumps, creating large hedges, or draping banks. The very fragrant, semi-double, blush-pink flowers are borne in large clusters, in a single long-lasting flush. The leaden green leaves create an interesting foil for the flowers, which appear in numerous clusters.

It is best seen on its own, when its interlacing branches can be fully appreciated.

'Snow Carpet'

Height: 45cm (18in)
Spread: 1.5–1.8m (5–6ft)
Like a few other Modern Shrubs, such as 'Raubritter' and 'Scintillation', this low-growing rose can be used to create colourful and unusual ground cover. It forms a closely packed mound of small, fully double, clear white, miniature flowers throughout summer. It is of a size that enables it to be grown in most gardens.

Other recommended Modern Shrub Roses:

'Ballerina'	'Marguerite Hilling'
'Bloomfield Abundance'	'Martin Frobisher'
'Dentelle De Malines'	'Mas Graf'
'Golden Chersonese'	'Nozomi'
'Heidelberg'	'Raubritter'
'Karl Förster'	'The Fairy'

Old Roses

Within this all-embracing classification are those roses that originated from hybrids and sports before the introduction of the Hybrid Teas. Many date back hundreds of years, some becoming curiosities of the rose world and others taking their places as distinctive and garden-worthy plants.

The major groups of Old Roses are Alba, Bourbon, Damask, Dwarf Polyantha, Gallica, Hybrid Musk, Hybrid Perpetual, Hybrid Rugosa, Hybrid Sweetbriar, Moss, Portland, Provence or Cabbage Roses and Scotch Roses.

'Adam Messerich'

'Adam Messerich'
Height: 1.8m (6ft)
Spread: 1.5m (5ft)
A superbly coloured Bourbon type, this rose was introduced in 1920. It has semi-double, rich pink flowers that reveal a raspberry-like fragrance. They retain their colour and are borne amid attractive leaves. The growth is vigorous and the plant is bushy, creating a dominant display. Flowering begins in early summer to midsummer and continues to the frosts of autumn.

'Alba Maxima'
Height: 1.8m (6ft)
Spread: 1.5m (5ft)
Widely known as the Jacobite Rose, Great Double White and Cheshire Rose, this magnificent Alba shrub creates a dominant display of highly scented, ivory-white, double, slightly untidy flowers that are blush tinted at first, later assuming creamy white shades. Flowering is early in midsummer, amid large bunches of lead-green leaves.

'Alba Maxima'

The related *alba semiplena* is thought to be the White Rose of York and bears very fragrant milk-white flowers. It is the rose used in the distillation of attar of roses in Bulgaria.

'Baron Girod de l'Ain'
Height: 1.5m (5ft)
Spread: 1.2m (4ft)
Introduced in 1897, this Hybrid Perpetual is a strikingly attractive rose, with large, initially cupped, richly scented, dark crimson flowers that open wide to create a saucer-shape. The petals are edged in white, creating a distinctive bloom, somewhat reminiscent of 'Roger Lambelin', an introduction made about seven years before this rose.

'Baronne Prévost'
Height: 1.5m (5ft)
Spread: 1.2m (4ft)
Introduced in 1842, this exquisite Hybrid Perpetual makes a very reliable shrub. The deep rose-pink flowers assume slightly lighter tones as the season progresses. Initially

'Baronne Prévost'

'Baron Girod de l'Ain'

'Belle de Crécy'

'Blanc Double de Coubert'

globular, the flowers open flat and are scented. In Victorian times, this and other roses of its type were very popular.

'Belle de Crécy'
Height: 1.2m (4ft)
Spread: 90cm (3ft)
This eye-catching Gallica forms a nearly thornless bush, with lax but strong arching stems. During midsummer it reveals fragrant, fully double flowers, purple-red in colour and maturing to a soft Parma-violet, with button-like eyes.

Gallicas are perhaps the oldest roses. They form short, neat, bushy shrubs with numerous tiny, hairy bristles but almost no thorns. They thrive in poor soils, but must not be planted in shade.

'Blanc Double de Coubert'
Height: 1.8m (6ft)
Spread: 1.5m (5ft)
This superb hybrid of *Rosa rugosa* was introduced in 1892. It has remarkable flowers with the texture of paper. The blooms are large, semi-double, pure white, and appear from early to late summer. They are tinted a slight blush when in bud. In autumn, the foliage becomes slightly yellow, with large, orange-red hips appearing. The growth is open, tall and lax, densely packed with prickles and with dark, deeply veined leaves.

'Camaieux'
Height: 120cm (4ft)
Spread: 90cm (3ft)
This magnificent Gallica was introduced in 1830 and is now highly prized by rosarians. At every stage, from buds to fully open flowers, it is distinctive and eye-catching. The white flowers, appearing in midsummer, are heavily splashed and striped with crimson. As the fragrant flowers mature, the stripes fade, first to magenta and then to soft lilac-grey. Although a relatively weak-growing plant, it still makes a lovely addition to the rose garden.

The 1846 introduction 'Tricolore de Flandre' is similar, with double, blush-white, fragrant flowers, and is attractive in a border.

'Cardinal de Richelieu'
Height: 1.5m (5ft)
Spread: 1.2m (4ft)
This rose is an 1840 Gallica Hybrid, and is unsurpassed for its sumptuous beauty. The dusky, dark purple flowers reflex almost into a ball. It has a slight fragrance, with dark green, smooth and shiny leaves that create an attractive foil for the midsummer flowers. It does require special attention: generous feeding and regular thinning and pruning. The extra attention is fully rewarded.

It is one of many roses that is recommended for all gardens. To rosarians this rose is known as 'The Blue Rose of the Arabs'.

'Camaieux'

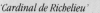
'Cardinal de Richelieu'   'Cécile Brunner'

'Chapeau de Napoleon'

'Charles de Mills'

'Comte de Chambord'

'Comtesse de Murinais'

'Cécile Brunner'

Height: 90cm (3ft)
Spread: 90cm (3ft)

Also known as 'Mignon', 'Madame Cécile Brunner' and the 'Sweetheart Rose', this Dwarf Polyantha is claimed by devotees of China Roses as well as those with admiration for Polyanthas. It was introduced in 1881 from a cross between *Rosa multiflora* and 'Madame de Tartas'. The miniature flowers have the nature of Hybrid Teas, and are blush-pink, often no larger than a thimble. It further excels in having a sweet fragrance. The flowers, which appear throughout summer, are borne amid dark green, pointed leaves. It has a short-jointed nature and does not require extensive pruning. There is also a climbing form.

'Chapeau de Napoleon'

Height: 1.5m (5ft)
Spread: 1.2m (4ft)

A superb Centifolia, this rose is also known as 'Centifolia Cristata' and 'Crested Moss', and was introduced in 1827. It is botanically known as *Rosa centifolia cristata* and produces richly fragrant, pure pink and slightly drooping flowers during midsummer. It has the added attraction of a frill of greenery around each bud.

'Charles de Mills'

Height: 1.5m (5ft)
Spread: 1.2m (4ft)

A strong-growing Gallica, often known as 'Bizarre Triomphant', this rose bears gloriously fragrant, densely packed, rich crimson flowers with a hint of purple as they age. They are unique, having a sliced-off appearance and are borne during midsummer amid dark green leaves. It is ideal for those people who have an aversion to thorns, as it is almost thornless.

'Comte de Chambord'

Height: 120cm (4ft)
Spread: 90 cm (3ft)

Introduced in 1860, this is a Portland Rose. Although few in this group are still grown, this is one that merits inclusion in the garden. Indeed, its stature is small enough to ensure that room could be made for it. The large, fragrant flowers are warm pink in colour with a hint of lilac, and have many rolled-back petals opening flat. This rose brightens gardens with colour throughout summer, and has good fragrance.

'Comtesse de Murinais'

Height: 1.8m (6ft)
Spread: 1.2m (4ft)

This magnificent Moss Rose was introduced in 1843 and has been widely grown ever since. The fully petalled flowers are blush-pink, opening flat and fading to white. Each flower is quilled and quartered, with a green button-like eye. Additionally, the flowers are sweetly fragrant. It is strong-growing and vigorous, and demands plenty of space.

'Cornelia'
Height: 1.5m (5ft)
Spread: 1.5m (5ft)
A vigorous and spreading Hybrid Musk, 'Cornelia' was introduced in 1925, and has been popular ever since. It bears its flowers mainly in early summer, and then intermittently until autumn. The blooms are small, rosette-shaped, and a coppery apricot in colour, fading to coppery pink. They are borne in large trusses and are especially fragrant; the scent is markedly carried on the air. Dark green leaves create a foil for the flowers. It can be planted in a shrub border or to form a hedge.

'Empress Josephine'
Height: 90cm (3ft)
Spread: 90cm (3ft)
Also known as 'Francofurtana' and introduced sometime before 1835, this Gallica Hybrid is frequently and colloquially known as the Frankfort Rose. The blooms are outstanding, perhaps the finest in the Gallica group. Large, clear, rich pink flowers are veined in deeper shades and are double and cup-shaped. It is not known for its scent, but does bear hips and is vigorous.

'Fantin Latour'
Height: 1.8m (6ft)
Spread: 1.5m (5ft)
'Fantin Latour' is a superb Centifolia. It has full-petalled flowers which are cupped at first, and later become reflexing and revealing at their edges. The superb

colouring of the flowers is blush-pink which deepens to shell-pink at the centre. Flowering is during midsummer. It is a superb rose, with the bonus of a sweet scent.

When planted to flank a path, or at the back of a border with 'green' plants in front, it is very appealing. However, do not plant it to form a background for highly variegated ground-hugging plants, as they will then compete for attention.

'Ferdinand Pichard'
Height: 120cm (4ft)
Spread: 90cm (3ft)
A distinctive 1921 introduction, this rose is claimed by most authorities to be a Hybrid Perpetual, but by others as a Bourbon. It has a repeat-flowering nature and produces fully globular, pink flowers striped with purple and crimson. Additionally, the flowers are richly and sweetly scented, borne amid smooth and pointed leaves. Its size enables it to be incorporated into most shrub borders.

'Frau Dagmar Hastrup'
Height: 1.5m (5ft)
Spread: 1.5m (5ft)
Introduced in 1914, this Rugosa type of rose is also often listed in catalogues as 'Frau Dagmar Hartopp'. It forms a compact yet bushy shrub with stems covered in prickles. The single, clear pink flowers have creamy stamens. These are followed in autumn by dark red,

'Cornelia'

'Empress Josephine'

'Fantin Latour'

'Frau Dagmar Hastrup'

'erdinand Pichard'

'Gloire du Ducher'

'rau Karl Druschki'

rounded hips. Sometimes the hips appear with the last of the flowers.

Vigilance is needed when pruning it – always remove dead wood. It is suitable for forming an attractive hedge.

'Frau Karl Druschki'
Height: 1.2–1.5m (4–5ft)
Spread: 1.2m (4ft)
Usually listed as a Hybrid Perpetual, but occasionally as a Hybrid Tea, this rose was introduced in 1901 and has remained popular ever since. The growth is vigorous, bearing beautifully formed buds. The buds open to form double, pure white flowers with a hint of lemon-green at their centres. If this rose is lightly pruned and the growth is pinned down, an abundance of flowers will be produced. Regrettably, the flowers are not scented.

'Gloire du Ducher'
Height: 1.8–2.1m (6–7ft)
Spread: 1.2m (4ft)
This tall and lax Hybrid Perpetual was introduced in 1865. It can be grown as a Climber, but is better when planted in a shrub border to create a dominant feature. The large petal-packed flowers are eye-catching. First they are deep crimson, and then they turn to purple as the flowers open. The blooms are especially attractive in autumn and are highlighted by the dark green leaves. The flowers have the added attraction of being richly scented.

'Honorine de Brabant'
Height: 1.8m (6ft)
Spread: 1.8m (6ft)
This rose is thought to be a sport of the sweetly scented 'Commandant Beaurepaire', but being more vigorous and leaf-packed. It is a Bourbon and forms a large shrub, with pale pink flowers, spotted and striped with crimson and mauve. Flowering is in midsummer, and from then, intermittently. The blooms are loosely cupped and reveal a rich raspberry fragrance. This rose is ideal for introducing into a scented garden.

It usually forms a shrub that is slightly wider than it is high, so ensure that it is given plenty of space.

'Jacques Cartier'
Height: 120cm (4ft)
Spread: 90cm (3ft)
A vigorous Portland type, 'Jacques Cartier' was introduced in 1868. This rose flowers intermittently throughout the summer season. Although growing strongly, it has a compact nature, with light green leaves. Beautiful, large, rich pink flowers are quartered and have a green centre. They exhibit a richly sweet fragrance.

'Köenigin von Dänemarck'
Height: 1.5m (5ft)
Spread: 1.2m (4ft)
Also known as 'Queen of Denmark', this rose will enrich any garden. It was introduced in 1826 with an

'Honorine de Brabant'

'Jacques Cartier'

'Köenigin von Dänemarck'

'Lady Curzon'

'La Ville de Bruxelles'

'La Reine Victoria'

'Louise Odier'

Alba and a Damask in its parentage. It is classified under the Old Rose group of Albas. Its lax and open nature does not detract from the well-shaped, intense, scarlet pink flowers that slowly assume softer tones towards the outside of the petals. The midsummer flowers are densely packed with petals, and often have a button-like eye. Like most Albas, it is extremely hardy and able to withstand sometimes trying and adverse conditions.

This rose associates well with many other roses in gardens. It can be planted as a background for small types, such as Miniature Roses. When planted in front of the willow-leaved pear (*Pyrus salicifolia*), it is especially appealing.

'Lady Curzon'
Height: 1.8m (6ft)
Spread: 2.4m (8ft)
A 1901 introduction, this rose resulted from a cross between *Rosa rugosa rubra* and *Rosa macrantha*. It is often classified as a Rugosa but sometimes as a Macrantha. The large, single, crinkled, pink flowers shade to white at their centres, revealing beautiful cream-coloured stamens. The scented flowers, often more than 7.5cm (3in) wide, appear in midsummer.

'La Reine Victoria'
Height: 1.8m (6ft)
Spread: 90cm (3ft)
An 1872 introduction, 'La Reine Victoria' is classified as a Bourbon. It has shell-like, warm rose-pink flowers with a delicious and intense fragrance. The blooms are double and appear over a long season. The petals are arranged in a circle and therefore appear cup-shaped in form.

Unfortunately, the flowers are inclined to become stained in wet weather. It is an upright and vigorous shrub rose with narrow, smooth leaves.

'La Ville de Bruxelles'
Height: 1.5m (5ft)
Spread: 1.2m (4ft)
Introduced in 1849, this rose is classified as a Damask. It has rich green, luxurious leaves and exceptionally large, rich pink, full flowers with button-like eyes. The blooms open flat, with petals reflexing at their edges. Flowers become paler as they age. The flowers also have the bonus of being sweetly scented, and appear during midsummer.

'Louise Odier'
Height: 1.5m (5ft)
Spread: 1.2m (4ft)
Without a doubt, this 1851 introduction is one of the most attractive of all Bourbons. The beautifully formed, cupped flowers are full of evenly arranged, rich pink petals shaded with lilac. They also have the added attraction of a strong, deliciously sweet fragrance. Flowering is continuous throughout summer.

'Madame Hardy'
Height: 1.8m (6ft)
Spread: 1.5m (5ft)
A magnificent Damask, 'Madame Hardy' was introduced in 1832 and is famed for its glorious, pure white flowers. The blooms are cup-shaped when they open and later become flat. While the outer edges of the petals turn down, the inner ones stay incurved. The flowers are blush-tinted when in bud, with a hint of a lemon scent.

This Old Rose is superb for creating a focal point in a border, where its pristine flowers will be seen to best advantage.

'Madame Isaac Pereire'
Height: 2.1m (7ft)
Spread: 1.5m (5ft)
This is a tall and vigorous Bourbon type, introduced in 1881. The large flowers are cupped and a deep madder-crimson in colour. They have a rich raspberry fragrance. Unfortunately, early flowers are often misshapen, but later ones are superb. Sometimes it is grown as a Climber for decorating pillars, as well as for covering walls.

It forms an attractive combination with many other flowers, including lilac, double paeonies, tulips and lilies.

'Madame Pierre Oger'
Height: 1.5m (5ft)
Spread: 90cm (3ft)
This Bourbon, introduced in 1878, is a sport of 'La Reine Victoria', to which it bears some resemblance except for the colour of its flowers. The flowers are pale silvery pink, shell-like, double and globular. They are also richly scented.

'Madame Plantier'
Height: 1.5–1.8m (5–6ft)
Spread: 1.8m (6ft)
An 1835 introduction, this rose is sometimes claimed as an Alba Rose or alternatively as a Noisette. Flowers are medium-sized, very sweetly scented, pompon-shaped, and creamy white. They are borne on gracefully arching shoots. The flowers are flushed a lemon colour at their centres when they first open, and they appear mainly during midsummer. Growth is dense, with shoots covered with small, light green leaves.

It can be grown as a Climber, reaching 3.5m (12ft) high, but is best seen as a shrub in a border.

'Maiden's Blush'
Height: 1.5m (5ft)
Spread: 1.2m (4ft)
A superb and very old Alba, 'Maiden's Blush' was known to be in existence before the fifteenth century. Semi-double, superbly and sweetly scented, blush-pink flowers appear during midsummer. These are borne amid greyish leaves on strong, arching stems. Without a doubt, it is one of the best garden roses, and well deserves a place in all rose gardens.

'Madame Hardy'

'Madame Isaac Pereire'

'Madame Pierre Oger'

'Madame Plantier'

'Maiden's Blush'

'Maréchal Davoust'

'Mutabilis'

'Maréchal Davoust'
Height: 1.2m (4ft)
Spread: 1.2m (4ft)
This well-known Moss Rose was introduced in 1853. It bears brownish, mossy buds that open to reveal large, cup-shaped, fragrant, intense carmine-pink flowers. The blooms gradually turn to lilac and purple. The stems and branches, like all Moss Roses, are densely covered with bristles. Flowering occurs mainly during midsummer.

'Mutabilis'
Height: 2.4m (8ft)
Spread: 1.8m (6ft)
The origin of this rose is uncertain. It is mainly listed as a China Rose but is also said to be, botanically, *Rosa × odorata* 'Mutabilis'. However, it certainly has *Rosa chinensis* as one of its parents. It was once known as 'die Turkische Rose', on the assumption it derived from *R. turkestanica*. Whatever its parentage, it undoubtedly is attractive and has the perpetual-flowering nature of a China type. Indeed, it is often still in flower in early winter.

The flame-coloured and pointed buds open to reveal chamois-yellow flowers that fade to pink and eventually to a coppery crimson. The copper-coloured foliage is sometimes damaged by severe and cold weather, and therefore is best planted in a sheltered position where the soil has been enriched.

'Nyveldt's White'
Height: 1.5m (5ft)
Spread: 1.2m (4ft)
This Rugosa Hybrid,
introduced in 1955, has
several species in its
parentage – *Rosa rugosa*,
Rosa majalis and *Rosa nitida*.
It forms an attractive shrub.
Large, single, pure white
flowers with pointed petals
are highlighted by the
stamens. Flowering is
mainly during midsummer,
with intermittent
appearances later. The
flowers reveal an
appealingly sweet
redolence, and are followed
by orange-red hips.

'Old Blush'
Height: 60cm–2.4m (2–8ft)
Spread: 1.8m (6ft)
Also known as the 'Old
Blush China', 'Blush China',
'Common Blush', 'Blush
Monthly Rose' and 'The
Monthly Rose', this China
Rose gains its names from
the regularity of its blooms.
The graceful clusters of pale
pink flowers, crimson-tinted
when in bud, often appear
up until early winter. With
age, these loosely formed
flowers assume deeper
tones. It is also fragrant.

When planted against a
warm wall it can often grow
up to 2.4m (8ft) tall.

It is said by some
rosarians to be the original
pink 'Bengal' rose which
was introduced from
Calcutta in 1790, and it is
certain that a rose of this
description has been grown
in China for more than one
thousand years.

'Nyveldt's White'

'Old Blush'

'Perle d'Or'

'Penelope'

'Petite de Hollande'

'Petite Lisette'

'Reine des Violettes'

'Penelope'
Height: 1.8m (6ft)
Spread: 1.5–1.8m (5–6ft)
A sturdy and popular Hybrid Musk, 'Penelope' was introduced in 1924. The semi-double flowers are rich creamy pink on opening, but fade later. They are highlighted by yellow stamens and have a delicious musky fragrance. In summer they are borne in small clusters, but the clusters are much larger in autumn. A bonus is the small, coral-pink hips covered with a grey bloom.

The growth is robust and vigorous, bearing broad, dark green leaves.

'Perle d'Or'
Height: 90cm–1.5m (3–5ft)
Spread: 90cm (3ft)
This rose was introduced in 1883, from a cross between a seedling of *Rosa multiflora* and 'Madame Falcot'. It is a Dwarf Polyantha and bears a resemblance to 'Cécile Brunner'. It is a delightful rose with Hybrid Tea-shaped blooms. The flowers are a warm rich apricot when in bud and fade almost to light, creamy salmon-pink when open. They appear almost perpetually throughout summer, with the added quality of a sweet musk-like fragrance.

'Petite de Hollande'
Height: 1.2m (4ft)
Spread: 90cm (3ft)
Introduced before 1802, this Centifolia is descended from *Rosa centifolia* but is often classified as a Provence or Cabbage Rose because of its more compact nature. It is a beautiful small-flowered shrub with pale pink flowers. The blooms deepen in colour toward the edges and are very fragrant. Flowering is mainly during midsummer.

'Petite Lisette'
Height: 1.2m (4ft)
Spread: 90cm (3ft)
This is a delightfully small Damask, which was introduced in 1817 but is still superb in today's shrub borders. The rounded, downy grey leaves become hidden in midsummer when the clear, light pink flowers emerge. The flowers have the added bonus of being scented. The petals radiate from a pronounced button eye.

'Reine des Violettes'
Height: 1.2–1.5m (4–5ft)
Spread: 90cm–1.5m (3–5ft)
Introduced in 1860, this rose is usually placed among the Hybrid Perpetuals, although it might be more usefully grouped with the Bourbons. Whatever its parentage and historical leanings, it is a superb variety. The deliciously scented flowers are in varying shades of purple and lilac, and are large and full. The flowers open flat, are quartered and have a button-like eye. Flowering is repeated throughout the summer and into autumn. Almost thornless stems and greyish leaves add to the attraction.

'Roseraie de l'Hay'

Height: 1.8–2.1m (6–7ft)
Spread: 1.5–2.1m (5–7ft)
This is a well-known 1901 introduction. It creates a dense and vigorous shrub, with shoots densely covered with prickles and glossy, dark green, deeply veined leaves. The rich, wine-purple, elongated flower buds open to reveal crimson-purple, velvety textured, double flowers, often in excess of 10cm (4in) wide. They are further enhanced by creamy stamens and a rich scent. It is a rose that creates an attractive feature when planted with its closely associated white varieties.

'Sarah Van Fleet'

Height: 1.8–2.4m (6–8ft)
Spread: 1.5–1.8m (5–6ft)
This rose is a superb Rugosa Hybrid, introduced in 1926 from a cross between *Rosa rugosa* and 'My Maryland'. Its long buds open to form semi-double, richly scented, flat flowers in a majestic, clear mallow-pink colour. The flowers are further enhanced by creamy stamens. Flowering occurs throughout summer and into autumn.

'Souvenir de la Malmaison'

Height: 1.5m (5ft)
Spread: 1.5m (5ft)
This magnificent Bourbon was introduced in 1843. The flowers are cupped at first, and later become flat. They are up to 13cm (5in) wide. The colouring is an exquisite soft pink which, with age, slightly fades. It flowers repeatedly during summer. It is often grown as a Climber, and, when trained to do so, frequently reaches 3m (10ft).

'Stanwell Perpetual'

Height: 1.5m (5ft)
Spread: 1.2–1.5m (4–5ft)
This is a Scotch Rose, introduced in 1838. It was said to have been found in a garden at Stanwell, just west of London. Parentage is uncertain, but it is thought to have been derived from a cross between *Rosa pimpinellifolia* and a Damask Rose. Some authorities suggest it is a hybrid from a cross between *R. pimpinellifolia* and *R. damascena*. Whatever its parentage, it is a hardy and suckering shrub, with grey-green leaves and very sweetly scented, saucer-

'Roseraie de l'Hay'

'Sarah Van Fleet'

'Souvenir de la Malmaison'

'Stanwell Perpetual'

Other recommended Old Roses:

'Amy Robsart'	'Félicité Permentier'	'Nuits de Young'
'Baroness Rothschild'	'Gloire des Mousseaux'	'Paul Crampel'
'Belle Isis'	'Hermosa'	'Robert le Diable'
'Boule de Neige'	'Jenny Duval'	'Rose de Resht'
'Celsiana'	'Lady Penzance'	'Soupert et Notting'
'Day Break'	'Louis Gimard'	'Vanity'
'De Meaux'	'Marie Louise'	'William Lobb'

'Tour de Malakoff'

'Tuscany Superb'

shaped, semi-double blush-pink flowers, which fade to white. The flowers appear initially in small clusters during early summer and midsummer, then repeatedly throughout the duration of summer.

'Tour de Malakoff'
Height: 1.8m (6ft)
Spread: 1.5m (5ft)
This vigorous, somewhat sprawling Centifolia was introduced in 1856. It has proved to be one of the greatest joys in the rose world. The large, paeony-like, scented flowers appear during midsummer. Their colouring is exquisite, first magenta-purple, then turning to a rich Parma-violet, and later to lavender and grey. Its lax nature needs support. Encourage it to grow up a pillar for a spectacular effect. Light shade does not appear to harm it.

'Tuscany Superb'
Height: 1.2–1.5m (4–5ft)
Spread: 60–90cm (2–3ft)
Also known as 'Superb Tuscany', this Gallica was introduced in 1848. It is more vigorous than 'Tuscany', the Old Velvet Rose, which was introduced in 1800. It is also reputed to be a sport of 'Tuscany'. However, it is less bushy and a little taller. The semi-double, deep crimson flowers fade to purple. Additionally, the flowers are slightly fragrant and followed by hips.

Rose Colours & Scented Roses

There are many varied colours of roses, from traditional deep red to vibrant bicolours. Some roses are solidly one colour, while others are formed of different shades. Many roses have colours that change as they open and mature or have a contrasting colour deep at the base of the petals.

Botanical interpretations of colours vary widely. For instance, the Floribunda 'Orangeade' has been variously described as light vermilion, brilliant orange-vermilion, bright vermilion-orange and golden orange with a luminous sheen. Additionally, the perceived colour is strongly influenced by the degree of sunlight: in low and decreasing light, dark colours darken more rapidly than light ones; conversely, in strong sunlight, light colours bleach faster than dark ones. Also, remember that perfect

colour recognition is rare, and that up to six per cent of all males have difficulty interpreting colours in the red and green spectrum, a problem that affects less than one per cent of females.

The roses here have been arranged in several colour groups, but, as many have varying tones or change with maturity, these can only be guides. The roses under the mixed colour listing have strikingly different colours rather than a gradual merging of shades.

All the roses here are scented, with the exception of those designated with an asterisk (*). Most scented roses have a sweet redolence, but some have the bouquet of raspberries, sweetbriar or lemon. Specific redolences are indicated under each individual entry in the glossary section.

WHITE

'Alba Maxima'
OLD ROSE
'Albéric Barbier'
RAMBLER
'Blanc Double de Coubert'
OLD ROSE*
'Bobby James'
RAMBLER
'Cinderella'
MINIATURE
'Frau Karl Druschki'
OLD ROSE*
'Iceberg'
FLORIBUNDA/CLIMBER
'Isis'
FLORIBUNDA
'Madame Alfred Carrière'
CLIMBER
'Madame Hardy'
OLD ROSE
'Madame Plantier'
OLD ROSE
'Margaret Merrill'
FLORIBUNDA
'Message'
HYBRID TEA*
'Nevada'
MODERN SHRUB ROSE*
'Nyveldt's White'
OLD ROSE
'Pascali'
HYBRID TEA*
'Pour Toi'
MINIATURE
Rosa banksiae
SPECIES ROSE
Rosa pimpinellifolia
SPECIES ROSE
'Snow Ball'
MINIATURE*

'Snow Carpet'
MODERN SHRUB ROSE*
'Wedding Day'
RAMBLER
'White Cockade'
CLIMBER
'White Pet'
FLORIBUNDA
'Yvonne Rabier'
FLORIBUNDA

YELLOW

'Amber Queen'
FLORIBUNDA
'Apricot Nectar'
FLORIBUNDA*
'Arthur Bell'
FLORIBUNDA
'Bright Smile'
FLORIBUNDA*
'Buccaneer'
HYBRID TEA*
'Dutch Gold'
HYBRID TEA
'Frühlingsgold'
MODERN SHRUB ROSE
'Golden Showers'
CLIMBER
'Golden Wings'
MODERN SHRUB ROSE
'Gold Pin'
MINIATURE*
'Grandpa Dickson'
HYBRID TEA*
'Joseph's Coat'
CLIMBER*
'King's Ransom'
HYBRID TEA
'Korresia'
FLORIBUNDA

'Lady Hillingdon, Climbing'
CLIMBER
'Mermaid'
CLIMBER
'Moon Maiden'
FLORIBUNDA
'Mountbatten'
FLORIBUNDA
'Mutabilis'
OLD ROSE*
'Peace'
HYBRID TEA
'Peer Gynt'
HYBRID TEA
Rosa foetida
SPECIES ROSE*
Rosa hugonis
SPECIES ROSE*
Rosa xanthina
SPECIES ROSE*
'Rosina'
MINIATURE
'Summer Sunshine'
HYBRID TEA
'Sutter's Gold'
HYBRID TEA

ORANGE

'Arcadian'
FLORIBUNDA
'Baby Darling'
MINIATURE*
'Baby Sunrise'
MINIATURE*
'Bonfire Night'
FLORIBUNDA*
'Colibri'
MINIATURE*
'Darling Flame'
MINIATURE

'Golden Slippers'
FLORIBUNDA
'Irish Mist'
FLORIBUNDA*
'Just Joey'
HYBRID TEA
'Lolita'
HYBRID TEA
'Mojave'
HYBRID TEA
'Orangeade'
FLORIBUNDA*
'Peek-a-Boo'
MINIATURE*
'Schoolgirl'
CLIMBER
'Troika'
HYBRID TEA
'Whisky Mac'
HYBRID TEA
'Young Venturer'
FLORIBUNDA

PINK

'Adam Messerich'
OLD ROSE
'Albertine'
RAMBLER
'Aloha'
MODERN SHRUB ROSE
'American Pillar'
RAMBLER*
'Angela Rippon'
MINIATURE
'Baby Masquerade'
MINIATURE
'Bantry Bay'
CLIMBER
'Baronne Prévost'
OLD ROSE

'Blessings'
HYBRID TEA
'Bobby Charlton'
HYBRID TEA
'Cécile Brunner'
OLD ROSE/CLIMBER
'Cerise Bouquet'
MODERN SHRUB ROSE
'Chapeau de Napoleon'
OLD ROSE
'Chicago Peace'
HYBRID TEA
'Circus'
FLORIBUNDA
'City of Leeds'
FLORIBUNDA
'Compassion'
CLIMBER
'Comte de Chambord'
OLD ROSE
'Comtesse de Murinais'
OLD ROSE
'Constance Spry'
MODERN SHRUB ROSE
'Cornelia'
OLD ROSE
'Dorothy Perkins'
RAMBLER*
'Elizabeth of Glamis'
FLORIBUNDA
'Empress Josephine'
OLD ROSE*
'Fantin Latour'
OLD ROSE
'Ferdinand Pichard'
OLD ROSE
'Francois Juranville'
RAMBLER
'Frau Dagmar Hastrup'
OLD ROSE*
'Fritz Nobis'
MODERN SHRUB ROSE
'Frühlingsmorgen'
MODERN SHRUB ROSE
'Galway Bay'
CLIMBER
'Helen Traubel'
HYBRID TEA
'Jacques Cartier'
OLD ROSE
'Köenigin von Dänemarck'
OLD ROSE
'La Reine Victoria'
OLD ROSE
'La Ville de Bruxelles'
OLD ROSE
'Lady Curzon'
OLD ROSE
'Lady Sylvia'
HYBRID TEA
'Lavender Jewel'
MINIATURE*
'Louise Odier'
OLD ROSE
'Madame Grégoire Staechlin'
CLIMBER
'Madame Pierre Oger'
OLD ROSE
'Maiden's Blush'
OLD ROSE

'Maréchal Davoust'
OLD ROSE
'Mullard Jubilee'
HYBRID TEA
'Nymphenburg'
MODERN SHRUB ROSE
'Old Blush'
OLD ROSE
'Parade'
CLIMBER
'Paddy McGredy'
FLORIBUNDA
'Penelope'
OLD ROSE
'Petite de Hollande'
OLD ROSE
'Petite Lisette'
OLD ROSE
'Pink Parfait'
FLORIBUNDA
'Pink Peace'
HYBRID TEA
'Prima Ballerina'
HYBRID TEA
'Queen Elizabeth'
FLORIBUNDA
Rosa californica
SPECIES ROSE
Rosa centifolia
SPECIES ROSE
Rosa gallica
SPECIES ROSE*
Rosa rubiginosa
SPECIES ROSE
Rosa rugosa
SPECIES ROSE
'Royal Highness'
HYBRID TEA
'Royal Salute'
MINIATURE
'Sarah Van Fleet'
OLD ROSE
'Scented Air'
FLORIBUNDA
'Scintillation'
MODERN SHRUB ROSE
'Sea Pearl'
FLORIBUNDA
'Shot Silk'
HYBRID TEA
'Silver Jubilee'
HYBRID TEA
'Souvenir de la Malmaison'
OLD ROSE*
'Stanwell Perpetual'
OLD ROSE
'Sweet Fairy'
MINIATURE
'Zephirine Drouhin'
CLIMBER

RED

'Alec's Red'
HYBRID TEA
'Belle de Crécy'
OLD ROSE
'Bettina'
HYBRID TEA

'Chelsea Pensioner'
MINIATURE*
'Crimson Glory'
HYBRID TEA
'Danse du Feu'
CLIMBER*
'Dortmund'
CLIMBER*
'Europeana'
FLORIBUNDA
'Evelyn Fison'
FLORIBUNDA
'Fragrant Cloud'
HYBRID TEA
'Frensham'
FLORIBUNDA
'John Waterer'
HYBRID TEA
'Memento'
FLORIBUNDA
'Mrs Sam McGredy'
HYBRID TEA
'Paradise'
HYBRID TEA
'Parkdirektor Riggers'
CLIMBER
'Perle d'Alcanada'
MINIATURE*
'Red Devil'
HYBRID TEA
'Red Lion'
HYBRID TEA*
Rosa moyesii
SPECIES ROSE*
'Rose Gaujard'
HYBRID TEA
'Rosemary Rose'
FLORIBUNDA
'Roseraie de l'Hay'
OLD ROSE
'Souvenir de Claudius Denoyel'
CLIMBER
'Starina'
MINIATURE
'Super Star'
HYBRID TEA
'Sarabande'
FLORIBUNDA
'Scarlet Fire'
MODERN SHRUB ROSE
'The Times Rose'
FLORIBUNDA
'Trumpeter'
FLORIBUNDA
'Satchmo'
FLORIBUNDA
'Wendy Cussons'
HYBRID TEA

CRIMSON

'Altissimo'
CLIMBER*
'Baron Girod de l'Ain'
OLD ROSE
'Charles de Mills'
OLD ROSE
'Christian Dior'
HYBRID TEA*

'Chrysler Imperial'
HYBRID TEA
'Crimson Glory, Climbing'
CLIMBER
'Crimson Shower'
RAMBLER*
'Ena Harkness'
HYBRID TEA
'Etoile de Hollande, Climbing'
CLIMBER
'Gloire du Ducher'
OLD ROSE
'Guinée'
CLIMBER
'Josephine Bruce'
HYBRID TEA
'Kronenbourg'
HYBRID TEA
'Lilli Marlene'
FLORIBUNDA
'Madame Issac Pereire'
OLD ROSE
'Mister Lincoln'
HYBRID TEA
'Papa Meilland'
HYBRID TEA
'Sympathie'
CLIMBER
'Tuscany Superb'
OLD ROSE

PURPLE

'Brown Velvet'
FLORIBUNDA*
'Cardinal de Richelieu'
OLD ROSE
'Intrigue'
FLORIBUNDA
'Reine des Violettes'
OLD ROSE
'Tour de Malakoff'
OLD ROSE

GREEN

'Green Diamond'
MINIATURE*

MIXED

'Camaieux'
OLD ROSE
'Double Delight'
HYBRID TEA
'Eye Paint'
FLORIBUNDA*
'Honorine de Brabant'
OLD ROSE
'Matangi'
FLORIBUNDA
'Old Master'
FLORIBUNDA
'Picasso'
FLORIBUNDA*
'Piccadilly'
HYBRID TEA
'Red Gold'
FLORIBUNDA

Rose Care

When planting bare-rooted roses, ensure that the bud union is just below the soil level and the roots are spread over a small mound of earth.

Planting

When properly planted, a rose will live for twenty or more years, but constricting the roots in poor soil is a recipe for disaster.

Thorough soil preparation is vital. Six to eight weeks before planting, dig the soil deeply, remove perennial weeds, and install drains if the site is constantly wet. A few weeks later, fork 135g per square metre (4oz per square yard) of bonemeal or special rose-planting fertilizer into the topsoil. Roses grow best in slightly acid soil, about pH 6.0 to 6.5. If the soil is more acid, dust with hydrated lime or ground limestone; if already chalky, dig out a large hole and replace with fresh soil.

Preparing the plant is also essential. Rose plants are either bare-rooted or container-grown. If bare-rooted, immerse the roots in a bucket of water for twelve hours, and if planting cannot take place immediately – the weather is too severe or the ground frozen or waterlogged – heel-in the plants in a shallow trench, covering and firming the roots with soil. Before planting, cut off dead roots and trim the rest back to 30cm (12in) long. Also cut off dead and thin shoots, as well as old leaves. Take care to keep the plant's label attached.

Container-grown roses should be placed in a freshly dug hole first, then their containers removed and soil trickled in around the plant.

Plant bare-rooted plants from late autumn to early winter, or in early spring. Dig a hole 60cm (2ft) wide and 25–30cm (10–12in) deep. Spread out the roots over a slight mound of soil, ensuring the bud union will be just below the surface when the soil settles. Firm soil in layers around the roots.

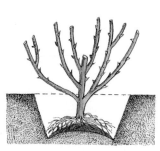

Plant container-grown types at any time when the soil is not dry, excessively wet or frozen. Prepare and improve the soil in the same way as for bare-rooted plants. Water the soil-ball before planting. After placing the plant in the hole, cut away the container. Trickle compost around the roots, then firm the soil.

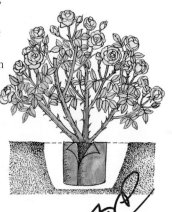

Mulching

Forming a 7.5cm (3in) thick layer of bulky organic material – peat, garden compost, decayed manure or leaf mould – around plants conserves soil moisture, prevents annual weeds growing, and improves and feeds the soil. It also reduces the risk of black spot disease.

Mulches are best applied in late spring, after the soil has warmed up. First remove all perennial weeds, fork in a spring dressing of fertilizers and thoroughly water the soil, then apply mulch. In autumn, mulch can be lightly forked into the surface soil.

Climbers need to be tied to a permanent structure, such as a trellis, for support.

Training

Bush roses usually need no support, although lax and spreading types benefit from several stout canes after a few years. Climbers need a permanent framework of wires or a trellis to which they can be tied. Pillar roses need a thick and stout pole for support, firmly secured in the ground, and Ramblers need an arch, pergola or trellis.

Feeding

To get the best – including a long life – from roses they need regular feeding with a balanced diet mainly of nitrogen, phosphate and potash, with smaller amounts of calcium and magnesium, and traces of iron, boron and manganese. The minerals must be in the right proportions and are therefore

best bought as proprietary mixtures.

For home gardeners, the best feeding routine is to apply a small handful of a general rose fertilizer around each plant in spring, before growth starts and leaves unfurl. Lightly fork fertilizer into the surface soil, then water. During early summer to midsummer, apply a further small handful. Do not feed after midsummer, as this encourages soft growth that is soon damaged in winter.

Established Hybrid Teas need to be pruned back to half their length each year in spring.

Pruning

Roses need to be regularly pruned. Each year they produce new growth, and if pruning is neglected the results will be fewer and smaller flowers and a tangled mass of shoots.

When to prune depends on the weather. Established roses are best pruned in early spring, when new growth is beginning. In cold regions this may be mid-spring, in warmer areas late winter or early spring.

In their first year, newly planted roses should be cut back severely: Hybrid Tea types to

Cut off dead flowers above the second or third leaf to promote new blooms.

13cm (5in) high; Floribundas to 15cm (6in); and Ramblers to 30cm (12in) high. Climbers just need the removal of dead tips.

Established roses in most gardens require 'moderate' pruning. Shoots on Hybrid Teas should be cut back to half their length. On Floribundas, new shoots close to the plant's base should be lightly pruned, but older ones cut to about 7–8cm (3in) of the plant's base. The method for Climbers and Ramblers depends on the variety, but, generally, Ramblers need all flowered shoots cut back to soil level in autumn and new shoots tied into place. Climbers need very little pruning other than cutting out old wood and reducing flowered stems to about 7.5cm (3in) long.

Cutting back long shoots in autumn reduces the risk of severe winter winds rocking plants and loosening roots. Cut with sharp secateurs so that snags are not left, as they encourage the entry of diseases. Make a sloping cut about 6mm (¼in) above an outward-pointing bud.

Watering

Although roses often have deep roots, many underachieve their

full potential through lack of water. However, once started, watering must be regular and thorough. Roses planted near walls need the most water, as well as newly planted types and those in light, sandy soils.

Dead-Heading

Cutting off dead flower heads from Hybrid Tea and Floribunda Roses ensures that the plant's energies are directed into subsequent growth, rather than the development of seeds and hips. Cut off dead flower clusters above the second or third leaf. Early flowers, which have faded, need to be removed with very little stem.

Cutting Roses for Decoration

Many roses are superb as cut flowers, but do not take them all from one plant. Also, when cutting the flowers, cut back to an outward-facing bud. Take flowers only from established plants.

Suckers should be removed below soil level and close to the roots.

Removing suckers

Sometimes shoots grow from the roots. As soon as they are seen, these suckers must be pulled off close to the roots. Remove soil so that the sucker is exposed, and replace it firmly after removal. Cutting a sucker off at ground level encourages further suckers.

Index

Figures printed in **bold** indicate illustrations.

Picture Credits

The publishers would like to thank the following photographers and agencies for the use of their pictures in this book. Pictures are credited on the page as follows: *(T)* **Top**, *(C)* **Centre**, *(B)* **Bottom**, *(TL)* **Top Left**, *(TR)* **Top Right**, *(CL)* **Centre Left**, *(CR)* **Centre Right**, *(CT)* **Centre Top**, *(CB)* **Centre Bottom**, *(BL)* **Bottom Left**, *(BR)* **Bottom Right**.

A-Z Botanical Collection: *2, 82(C), 83(T), 86(C), 88(T), 88(BL), 89(T), 89(CT), 90(T), 91(TR), 91(C), 92(C), 93(T), 93(C), 95(TL), 95(TR), 95(CL), 96(CL), 97(B), 98(T), 101(T), 103(T), 104(BL), 104(BR), 105(C), 106(C), 108(C), 108(BR), 109(T), 111(BR), 111(BL), 112(T), 112(CT), 113(B), 114(TR), 114(CR), 115(T), 117(TR), 118(T), 119(B), 123(C), 128(CT), 129(T), 130(T), 131(TL), 132(BL), 135(C), 140(B), 143(B), 144(BL), 145(B), 148(CR), 149(T), 150(CB).*

Ancient Art & Architecture Collection: *10(B), 20(T), 31(B).*

Ardea: *80.*

R. C. Balfour: *60, 83(T), 84(TL), 84(BR), 86(T), 87(BL), 89(B), 90(C), 91(B), 92(TR), 95(CR), 98(CT), 98(B), 100(BR), 102(C), 103(CL), 103(B), 105(T), 105(B), 106(T), 107(CR), 112(B), 114(B), 116(T), 118(CL), 119(T), 119(C), 122(CL), 124(B), 126(B), 127(T), 131(B), 137(T), 138(B), 140(T), 142(C), 143(TR), 143(CR), 147(CL), 147(B), 148(CL), 148(B), 150(T), 150(CT).*

The Bridgeman Art Library: *endpapers, 9(T), 11, 12-13, 14, 15(B), 20(B), 21, 23, 24, 27, 30, 31(T), 35.*

Eric Crichton Photos: *110(B), 120(B), 122(B), 123(B), 130(B), 132(T), 132(BR), 135(T), 142(T), 143(TL), 144(T), 144(BR), 145(T), 147(TR), 150(B).*

Fine Art Photographs: *8, 9(B), 25, 26, 28(T), 29, 32(B), 33, 36, 37(B).*

Michael Gibson: *16.*

Di Lewis © Salamander Books: *cover, 6-7, 40-59, 61-79.*

The Mansell Collection: *15(T), 19, 37(T).*

Mary Evans Picture Library: *22, 28(B), 34.*

Photos Horticultural Picture Library: *17(B), 38, 39, 128(T), 137(CB), 148(T).*

Harry Smith Horticultural Photographic Collection: *1, 17(T), 81, 82(T), 82(B), 83(B), 84(TR), 84(C), 84(BL), 85, 86(B), 87(T), 87(CR), 87(BR), 88(BR), 89(B), 90(B), 91(TL), 92(TL), 92(B), 93(B), 94, 96(TL), 96-97(T), 96(B), 97(C), 98(CB), 99, 100(TL), 100(TR), 100(C), 100(BL), 101(B), 102(T), 102(B), 103(CR), 104(T), 104(C), 106(B), 107(TL), 107(TR), 107(B), 108(TL), 108(TR), 108(BL), 109(B), 110(T), 111(T), 111(CR), 112(CB), 113(T), 114(TL), 114(CL), 115(B), 116(B), 117(TL), 117(CL), 117(CR), 117(B), 118(CR), 118(B), 120(T), 121, 122(TL), 122-123(T), 124-125(T), 124(C), 125, 126(TL), 126(TR), 126(C), 127(C), 127(B), 128(CB), 128(B), 129(B), 131(CL), 131(TR), 132(CL), 133, 134, 135(BL), 135(BR), 136(T), 136(B), 137(CT), 137(B), 138(T), 138(C), 139, 140(CL), 140(CR), 141, 142(B), 144(CL), 144(CR), 146, 147(TL), 147(CR), 149(C), 149(B), 151.*

Werner Forman Archive: *18.*

B. Wilson/Ancient Art & Architecture Collection: *10(T).*

Acknowledgements

Grateful acknowledgement is made to the following for permission to reproduce previously published material.

Roman recipes on page 11 and quote from Martial on page 1:
From *Through the Ages* by Gabriele Tergit, published by Oswald Wolff Books, Berg Publishers, 1961. Reprinted by permission of Oswald Wolff Books, Berg Publishers.

Rhymes on page 20:
From *Origins of Rhymes, Songs and Sayings* by Jean Harrowven. Published by Kaye and Ward, 1979. Reprinted by permission of Jean Harrowven.

Edmund Waller poem on page 29:
Excerpt from poem by Edmund Waller from *Benbary's Book of Quotations*. Reprinted by permission of Ward Lock, a division of Cassell plc.

Song lyrics on page 30:
"Roses Of Picardy" (Weatherby/Wood)
© Chappell Music Ltd.
Reproduced by permission of Warner Chappell Music Ltd.

'A rose is a rose is a rose' on page 30:
Gertrude Stein quotation from *The Reader's Encyclopaedia* by William Rose Benet, published in the U.K. by A.N.C. Black. Reprinted by permission of A.N.C. Black.

Many thanks to Valerie Lewis Chandler, BA, ALAA, for compiling the index for this book.